T0384587

128
Colors

Katrin Trautwein

128 Colors

A Sample Book for
Architects, Conservators, and
Designers

Birkhäuser
Basel

Dedicated to Susanne Hürlimann

6 Introduction

Chapter 1
16 The Whites

Chapter 2
52 The Grays and Blacks

Chapter 3
76 The Umbers

Chapter 4
102 The Bronzes and Metallics

Chapter 5
112 The Yellows

Chapter 6
126 The Ochers

Chapter 7
146 The Oranges

Chapter 8
162 The Reds

Chapter 9
180 The Red Ochers and Browns

Chapter 10
200 The Carmines, Violets, and Purples

Chapter 11
224 The Blues

Chapter 12
262 The Greens

Introduction

A few years ago, Susanne Hürlimann and I founded a small color factory. Our first, fundamental concern was a philosophical and an economic one: which colors should we produce? It was obvious that the colors would be designed for architecture, interiors, and facades. But which colors exactly?

In 1997, during one of my many literary research sessions, I stumbled upon a new edition of Le Corbusier's color keyboards with original color examples. His *Polychromie architecturale*[1] was at that point virtually unknown. The sheer beauty of the color chart, his restriction of the number of nuances to 63, and the name Le Corbusier as the crowning point, led me to Paris to the headquarters of the Fondation Le Corbusier, the administrating offices of Le Corbusier's estate. The Fondation Le Corbusier awarded our small company the rights to reproduce Le Corbusier's colors—despite, as it later turned out, competition from economically much more powerful companies. For me, this was the beginning of an adventurous journey into the history of colors in architecture. This publication is one of the results of this undertaking.

In the process of my research and color production work, it became clear to me that color is now interpreted and mixed differently than it was up until the 1950s. The following is a list of how color was approached differently in early modernism than it is today.

- The choice of pigments: aesthetics gave way to efficiency; each color including white is brighter and purer than in the past.

---

1 Arthur Rüegg (ed.), *Polychromie architecturale. Le Corbusiers Farbenklaviaturen von 1931 und 1959/ Le Corbusier's Color Keyboards from 1931 and 1959/ Les claviers de couleurs de Le Corbusier de 1931 et de 1959* (Basel, Boston, Berlin, 1997) (reprint, 2006).

- The systematization: today colors are merely analyzed and defined in the visible wavelength region extending from approx. 400 to 700 nm. Thus, the phenomenon of color is reduced to one value in a narrow range of the full energetic spectrum.
- The naming: series of numbers that relate to numerical or quantitative positions in a virtual color space have replaced names that convey meaning, such as "sky blue," or names derived from origin, such as "Venetian red" or "bone black" (a pigment made from charred bones). Color has become a question of location, not of substance and complex sensory perception.
- The psychological implications: before 1950, the aesthetic-spatial effect of a color still determined its use, and after 1950, the results of psychological studies of color perception became the decisive factor.
- The tradition in architecture and in painting: today, industrially manufactured ranges of colors reflect ease of production and price. Established artistic traditions are not given priority.

This publication introduces colors that are rooted in all of these historical aesthetic traditions. It presents a collection of 128 colors that are particularly useful for architecture, interior design, architectural preservation, and color design. The colors have been reproduced using a complex, four-color printing procedure, based on the highly pigmented Aniva® printing process. In addition, eight supplementary colors were printed individually. Information is provided about each color's origin or "author," as well as the specific historical usage, which differentiates it from all other colors. It is a "book of samples" with the cultural history of 128 colors, which can indeed be industrially manufactured, but their production is more complex than conventional color production. The introduction in this publication, and the thematic introductions that begin each chapter, provide a theoretical basis for questions concerning the use of color by architects, interior architects, monument conservationists, and designers. A forthcoming handbook will discuss each topic in more detail.[2]

Choosing Pigments

A short review of the origins of the colors used in architecture shows that colors are now chosen for different reasons than before 1920. At the beginning of industrialization, paint was chosen according to aesthetic considerations,

2 Katrin Trautwein, *Color as Material. A Handbook for Architects, Conservators, and Designers*, in production at Birkhäuser Verlag. Planned release: 2011.

and the limits of its use were defined primarily by the availability of the pigments. The discourse took place between the architect, the client, and the craftsman who mixed the pigment with binder, thus creating the paint.

In the process of industrialization, newly developed pigments such as cobalt green, mars yellow, and phthalocyanine blue flooded the market. Innovative technical manufacturing procedures brought down the cost of production. The process of manufacturing colors in the new factories, a process defined chiefly by economics, was given priority over aesthetic decisions. Chemists or factory owners have rarely been the best guardians of aesthetics, hence, color selection and the used pigments gradually became more efficient, purer, and brighter. This process still continues today.

The Systematization

There was another factor that made the discussion even more abstract: the color systems developed in 1900 by Albert Henry Munsell (1858–1918) and Wilhelm Ostwald (1853–1932).[3] The objective of their systems was to systemize and standardize the nomenclature in the industrial diversity of color, but these were also systems that allowed a large number of color shades to be defined on the basis of a small number of primary colors. The common belief that every conceivable *visible color* can be assigned to such a color system is unsustainable.[4] Because this color systemization could automate the mixing of standard pigments very precisely, it offered new possibilities of rationalization. The three-dimensional models behind Ostwald's and Munsell's color systems are composed of triangular single color surfaces, edged by black, white, and a full color. Between each are graduated nuances of mixed colors. These triangles are arranged upright around a central axis so that they form a color wheel (Ostwald) or an ellipse (Munsell), with the saturated full colors located at the edge, and a vertical black-white axis serving as the connecting central axis for all the triangles. All of the triangles together form the three-dimensional color space. A red-green and a yellow-blue axis run horizontally through the middle of the color wheel.

The path from such a color classification system to a reduction of the manifold pigments in use to a few which, due to their strength of color and purity, were best suited for simple mixing, was a short one. Pigments were searched for and found that behaved as monochromatically as possible, that is, the purest blue pigment possible, with no red or a green tint.

3 Narciso Silvestrini, Ernst-Peter Fischer and Klaus Stromer (eds.),
   Farbsysteme in Kunst und Wissenschaft (Cologne, 1998).
4 Friedrich Schmuck, "Farbsysteme und Farbordnungen," in *Farbe und Architektur*,
   Rainer Wick (ed.), *Kunstforum International* 57(1) 1983, p. 163–180.

Color classification systems break down a ruby red color, for instance, into in a mixture of black, white, and a bluish red. Light blue could be a composition made from:

- blue and white (pure light blue)
- blue with black and white (a muted light blue)
- blue with added green, black, and white (a muted, light blue color with a green tint)
- blue with added red, black, and white (a matt, light blue color with a violet tint).

For mathematical reasons, light blue cannot simultaneously be defined to have a red and a green tint. Color classification systems such as these compose every color from a maximum of two of four possible chromatic colors, and two nonchromatic colors.

However, colors in nature are generally composed of all six colors. To achieve the harmonious effect of natural pigments, color-mixing software has to be outmaneuvered. The missing colors have to be replaced by means of complementary admixtures (green to red, violet to yellow, and orange to turquoise). Left to its own devices, the software behind color-matching systems will not create the same effect as a natural pigment.

Names

A color's position on the color sphere can be determined by using three coordinates: using ruby red as an example, the coordinates first establish the distance of ruby red to a pure red on the perimeter of the color wheel; then they define the distance from the nonchromatic center, and third, its lightness or height on the black-white axis. A color system such as this is beneficial because it communicates information unambiguously, because it can be translated easily into color-matching software, and because the coordinates can be translated straightforwardly from one color system to another. Thus, Natural Color Systems' (NCS) color coordinates and those of Ostwald's color model can be translated into RGB monitor or CMYK print coordinates. In so doing, the position on the NCS color sphere is calculated and translated into the position on a second color sphere that is based on a different system of classification. Cultural and material differences become insignificant in the face of the mathematics involved in these operations, and the sensual references of color names, such as "velvet black," a traditional artists' name for ivory black pigment, disappear. Such a color culture aims to maximize reproducibility, not aesthetics.

Very few people were aware that, in fact, more and more nuances were being produced from less and less pigments. This is because the discourse around color became increasingly distanced from the coloring materials on which it was originally based. The growing gap between coloring materials and color knowledge remained invisible until the color was used to define architecture. It became evident in the increasingly bright, dull, flat, or artificial effects of the wall or facade paints used in our built and designed environment.

The Psychological Implications

Aesthetics were, of course, still being considered, but they were no longer based on the spatial effects of the coloring materials—simply because this knowledge was (and is) no longer commonly available. Psychological studies of color perception resulted in ostensibly substantiated conclusions about color effects, and these were assigned to positions on the 3d-color models. The psychological classification of dematerialized colors provided standardized colors with meaning. There were numerous publications that summarized the many studies, and identified generalized color effects that established themselves as the definitive criteria for choosing colors since the 1950s.[5] One example is the conclusion that "colors automatically trigger subconscious reactions and associations (that are partially archetypical, meaning, they are inherent and thus fundamental): blue is quieting, red is exciting or aggressive, yellow triggers fear."[6]

Such conclusions are not completely unjustified, but they are indiscriminate and reflect an inexact use of language. A deep blue made from ultramarine is, for instance, not very quieting at all. "Blue" is an abstract and broad term, as will be shown here. So, which blue does, in fact, trigger the above-mentioned color associations, and, under which lighting conditions, and with which surrounding colors? Answers to these and other similar questions can provide architects and designers with true guiding principles. The generalization of color effect to an entire color region, as is described in the above example with blue, is the result of neglecting to consider the intimate relationships between coloring materials and color perception. Feelings are now projected onto terms such as "blue," because the actual pigment

5 Three contemporary examples of these are: Eva Heller, *Wie Farben wirken. Farbpsychologie, Farbsymbolik, kreative Farbgestaltung* (Reinbek near Hamburg, 2004);
Ingrid Riedel, *Farben. In Religion, Gesellschaft, Kunst und Psychotherapie* (Stuttgart, 2009);
Klausbernd Vollmar, *Farben. Symbolik – Wirkung – Deutung* (Munich, 2009).
6 Vollmar, 2009, p. 15.

is an unknown. In modern design teachings, communication, which is an act of quantitative analysis, is equated with perception, which is a sensory process. The emotional response that a certain pigment might trigger is unknown in these teachings.

The perceptions of a subject, and the color as object, cannot be separated—this was Goethe's greatest realization. He was the first to realize that justice cannot be done to the phenomenon of color if it is not observed in its complex context of meanings. The first level of color meaning is purely individual-aesthetic, or subjective (what do I think is beautiful?). The second level of meaning is collective-cultural, or intersubjective (for what has this color been used, what symbolism is associated with this color?), and the third level is the objective one (what is measurable?). A choice of colors based only on what is measurable between 400 and 700 nm, thus neglecting the specific characteristics of pigments outside this realm, runs the risk of being arbitrary.

Traditions in Architecture and in Painting

To return from this world of arbitrary color, we turn to coloring materials and their history. With this in mind, this book pleads for an approach to color selection that considers color as a material. What happens if colors are selected again according to considerations of coloring materials and their history of use?

The collection of colors in this publication takes into account the rich compendium of cultural meaning that arose in the course of the human endeavor to create poetic and expressive paints.

Some colors develop a unique effect on a surface, due to the way in which they respond to light. This interaction with light is due to the pigments. Sulfur particles in the crystal core of ultramarine blue, for instance, transform invisible ultraviolet light into a unique blue color. It is why ultramarine blue is still luminous in dark spaces. Ultramarine blue, ultramarine green, Prussian blue, and colors made from bronze and vermilion all demonstrate a unique interplay of color and light, which makes them important and irreplaceable for color designers. And they are typically not even included in the conventional color classification systems! All colors in this book fulfill several of the following criteria:

– They are produced from pigments that have a special effect in light.

– They are important on a cultural-historical level; their use was
  established at a time when color aesthetics was held in high esteem.
– They develop a striking three-dimensional effect in space, one
  that cannot be imitated by other colors.
– They were used by a well-known architect or artist to successfully
  fulfill a certain purpose.
– They are found in nature, or are familiar to most people as an archetypical color experience, and are therefore considered particularly
  beautiful.

The Choice of Color

Just as Goethe rejected Isaac Newton's 1704 color system, understanding that the color phenomenon could not be divided into separate objective
and subjective realms, Le Corbusier also knew that he would not be doing
justice to the complex reality of color effects using Ostwald's color system.
Le Corbusier chose colors according to their pigments, and not according
to their location in an immaterialized color space. "Intelligence and passion;
there is no art without emotion, no emotion without passion."[7] Colors
that are chosen with intelligence and passion produce joy, create serene or
joyous atmospheres and enhance the three-dimensional effect of a room.
It is of great value to color research that Le Corbusier documented and
recorded his architecture-oriented color selection.[8] He believed that intelligence and emotion pointed in the same direction and developed a purist
scale of 43 colors that could be used to fulfill certain atmospheric and constructive functions by means of color.[9] His scale was based on 17 traditional
artistic pigments. These were divided into 14 groups of color nuances,
most of them comprised of a full tone and a small number of well-considered
pastel tones.

Le Corbusier's architecture changed around 1950. He exposed
concrete and other materials such as wood and steel, the inherent colors of
the material fulfilled the atmospheric function, and constructive relationships were highly visible. Color began to take on a decorative and compositional role. Alfred Roth aptly described the purpose of the second of
these color concepts with the expression, "compositional balance."[10]
The new Le Corbusier color scale required for these functions comprised
only 20 dominant colors.[11] The 63 colors of Le Corbusier's *Polychromie*

7 Le Corbusier, "Towards a New Architecture,"
  in *Essential Le Corbusier, L'Esprit Nouveau Articles*
  (Oxford, 1998), p. 164.
8 Rüegg, 1997 (reprint, 2006).
9 Le Corbusier, *Claviers de Couleurs Salubra* (Basel, 1931).
10 Rüegg, 1997 (reprint, 2006), p. 80.
11 Le Corbusier, *Claviers de Couleurs Salubra 2* (Basel, 1959).

architecturale together form a coherent, rationally justifiable, and highly aesthetic color system for architecture. These colors make up approximately half of the colors we have included in this book.

The other colors presented here cannot be summarized into a comparable group. They have different origins and underlying concepts. Some, such as Champagne white and Green tea, have become popular favorites, because they fulfill certain aesthetic desires. Others have been successfully employed by architects who work intensely with color as a design element in their architecture. Yet others are part of a classic palette with a long history of popularity which has, despite new developments, remained significant. Pompeian red is a perfect example here.

We have included classic colors that fulfill their task better than any other, or that are considered beautiful by many observers. The palette we are presenting here is the result of many years of experience working collaboratively with architects, interior architects, conservators, and designers.

We have endeavored to compile a rounded and balanced palette. The fundamental chapters, which are dedicated to the whites, the grays and blacks, and the umbers, are supplemented by chapters on other chromatic colors. All of the colors have proven to be highly compatible.

Nevertheless, a selection can and will never be complete, which is why I would appreciate any feedback, suggestions, additions, and arguments for or against the colors chosen for this series. This would fulfill a very important purpose: namely to reanimate the discourse involving color and architecture in theory and in practice. They belong together, to return to Goethe's realization.

Acknowledgements

I would first like to thank Susanne Hürlimann and my parents. Susanne made it possible for me to establish a company; my parents endowed me with curiosity and a first-class education. They are valuable gifts. I would also like to sincerely thank Thomas Fritz, who corrected many errors and spent numerous Sunday afternoons listening to ideas and unfinished thoughts.

I am indebted to Karoline Mueller-Stahl for the competent, humorous, and witty editorial work. I have often been amazed at chiseled sentences in other books, and now I know that they may not have been that chiseled when they arrived on the editor's desk, and that the editor first had to shape them. It was often the case with this publication. I would also like to thank the publishing house production manager, Werner Handschin, graphic artist Muriel Comby, and translator Laura Bruce, who share my passion for color. Sometimes you are fortunate enough to meet people that combine talent, skill, perfectionism, and humor. I found this here, and the collaboration was a pleasure.

A different type of acknowledgement goes to three companies that supported the costs of printing. The first is the artisanal paint manufacturer kt.COLOR that researches traditional paints and pigments and invents production methods for old and new color shades to make them safe, valuable, and beautiful. kt.COLOR sells the traditionally mixed pigmented paints presented in this book to an international clientele. The second is distributor Thymos AG, the Swiss distributor of the paints manufactured by kt.COLOR and other environmentally sound paints. The third is Karl Bubenhofer AG, also an innovative Swiss enterprise, that was the first company in the world to develop, in collaboration with kt.COLOR, industrial recipes for the complex, complementary mixed colors presented in this publication. These industrially pigmented paints can be purchased at KABE. Without their contribution, this book would have not been produced with the same quality.

Comparing a calm, beautiful color with a gourmet meal or a quality wine is justified, because they all directly influence our well-being. Of the three, however, the effect of a first-class color will be the most lasting. Which makes it even more astounding that we know so little about it! It would be wonderful if this book could contribute to a better understanding of the relationships between color and architecture.

A Short Instruction Manual
What Information Can Be Found in this Publication?

– 08.001 – A color number. Le Corbusier's colors have their own numbering system. The other colors follow a similar system.
– Champagne white – The traditional color name.
– Source – The author, the first or the most well-known user of a color, or the source of the sample used in formulating the new edition of the color.
– History – The origin and justifications of the color.
– Spatial qualities – Notes on possible functions or limits: whether the color stays in the background or asserts itself in space, whether it is particularly useful in conditions of either strong or low lighting. I will go into more depth about these architecturally significant factors in a forthcoming theoretical publication.[12]
– Historical pigmentation – The traditional pigmentation, as implemented by kt.COLOR.
– Industrial pigmentation – An alternative pigmentation produced industrially without the use of natural pigments, as manufactured in Switzerland, for example, by Karl Bubenhofer AG.
– Facade suitability – Notes on whether the color can be manufactured so as to be suitable for facades.
– CMYK approximation – The closest approximation to the color within the CMYK color system for print.[13]
– RGB approximation – The translation of the CMYK approximation into the RGB system for presenting color on a calibrated monitor screen.[14]

12 Trautwein, planned release 2011
13 Michael and Pat Rogondoni, *Process Color Manual.*
   24'000 CMYK Combinations for Design, Prepress and Printing,
   (San Francisco, 2000).
14 Adobe Systems, InDesign Version CS3, 2007.

The Whites

White evokes a variety of associations. It embodies the "virgin sheet of paper," the expansive room, untouched snow, and is the color of purity. It makes forms visible and is uncompromising in how it exposes architectural dimensions.

The popular association of the color white with modernist architecture and its ambitious efforts to create a functional aesthetic strangely overpowers the actual facts. The *Weißenhofsiedlung* housing estate in Stuttgart serves as an excellent example. Only one third of the numerous houses were, in fact, ivory white; Mies van der Rohe painted his house a light salmon, Bruno Taut's house was very colorful, and Ludwig Hilberseimer's was gray.[2] The fact that many now believe that the housing development was completely white and are determined to restore it to a pure, white state, which it never had in the first place, illustrates a denial of color and the mythic character of white.

Three tendencies have contributed to the phenomenon of white becoming an almost unquestioned symbol of modernity. Firstly, in modernism's attempts to overcome the decorative aesthetic of *Jugendstil*, Le Corbusier, Adolf Loos, and others extolled in various polemic essays the white wall as a pure art form and the embodiment of aesthetics. Secondly, the concept of the "white wall" is not the same as modernism's very "off-white" color. If modernism used white, it was the color of chalk or cream![3] Thirdly, the oft-debated subject of color in architecture, with its many non-quantifiable references, emotional connotations, and overtones of superficiality, was often willingly excluded from educational curricula, meaning that an important architectural element of design was neglected or opposed.

All this led to white being considered neutral, and allowed it to be used to cover large surfaces imprudently. White paints are not neutral and a white environment is not an empty space, it is a space filled with a specific white. Too much white will lead to optical over-stimulation. A white environment is so bright that the pupil must contract in order to reduce the amount of light entering the eye. Objects that are near a white surface will look duller and darker than they actually are. Choosing pure

"Paper, I understand, was invented by the Chinese; but western paper is to us no more than something to be used, while the texture of Chinese paper and Japanese paper gives us the feeling of warmth, or calm and repose. [...]
Western paper seems to turn away the light, while ours seems to take it in, to envelop it gently like the soft surface of a first snowfall. It gives off no sound when it is crumpled or folded, it is quiet and pliant to the touch as the leaf of a tree."
Tanizaki Jun'ichiro [1]

white for museums and exhibitions should absolutely be questioned! "That burst of light from those four walls hardly puts one in the mood to relish Sōseki's physiological delight."[4] Tanizaki Jun'ichiro is referring to the glaringly lit quality of rooms painted completely white.

White surfaces may scatter or reflect light, or do both—it depends on the particular white pigment and its granulation and crystal structure. The western paper so rebuked by Jun'ichiro scatters light, while Chinese paper reflects it. Warm and inviting white rooms are created by whites with a balanced color depth. Such whites are made with pigments not optimized for opacity, but for their light-reflective qualities. A white color can be chosen according to whether or not it is inviting, whether or not it seems appealing, or whether or not it is glaring.

Usually, the white pigments that are most in demand are efficient (meaning one coat of paint is enough), with small, opaque, amorphous, hard particles, and whose hue is as neutral as possible. White colors such as these, which are manufactured mainly from micronized titanium dioxide with or without a bit of carbon black, such as NCS 0500, are harshly white. The micronization of pigments optimizes a paint's hiding power by eliminating crystals, thereby promoting the diffusion or scattering of light from the white surface at the expense of reflection from crystal surfaces. This explains the aggressive character of many white surfaces.

A nice counter-example of this is the venerable Champagne chalk. It has a gentle, dry and distinct color, metaphorically similar to the taste of the king of wines; the pigment particles are large and archetypical, the surface texture velvety and inviting. These qualities create a subtle depth that embeds neighboring colors, people, and art works in a calm and gentle background.

1 Tanizaki Jun'ichiro, *In Praise of Shadows* (Tokyo, 1933 and New York, 2001), p. 9–10.
2 Mark Wigley, *White Walls, Designer Dresses. The Fashioning of Modern Architecture* (Cambridge and London 2001), p. 305.
3 "Entièrement blanche la maison serait un pot à crème." Le Corbusier, *Almanach de l'Architecture Moderne*, Collection de *L'Esprit Nouveau* (Paris 1926), p. 146.
4 See note 1, p. 6.

CMYK approximation:
0.3.8.2

RGB approximation:
249.244.233

Spatial qualities:
passive and stable under
all light conditions

Historical pigmentation:
Champagne chalk

Industrial pigmentation:
titanium white with
red oxide, yellow oxide, and
chrome green

Facade suitability:
weather-resistant in some
techniques

08.001

Champagne white / Blanc de craie de Champagne

A traditional white distemper paint until circa 1950

The French province of Champagne is famous for its soil rich in belemnite chalk, which gives the grapes from this region their characteristic tart, aromatic flavor. The soft chalk has a porous structure that retains moisture and stores warmth, and these in turn are fed into the vines. The chalk from Champagne was originally marketed as "Violette" and became one of the most popular chalks used in fine art painting. Its unique attributes make it opaque and pleasing. Its playful interaction with incoming waves of light lends it a remarkably soft light reflectance. The term "soft light reflectance" means that no discontinuities are present in the spectrum of the visible color between 400 to 700 nm. The beige color of Champagne white soothes the eyes like a landscape of gently rolling hills.

CMYK approximation:
0.0.5.0

RGB approximation:
255.254.246

Spatial qualities:
passive and stable under
all light conditions

Historical pigmentation:
Rügen chalk

Industrial pigmentation:
titanium white with approx.
0.5% umber

Facade suitability:
weather-resistant

32.000

White light / Blanc lumineux

A traditional white distemper paint until circa 1950

White light is comparable to the color of the most pure chalks, such as Rügen *Dreikronenkreide* [*three crown chalk*]. All chalk mines—such as the massive chalk cliffs of Champagne, the deposits in Crete (Latin: creta = chalk), or those in Bologna— possess a unique color quality that results from the yellow, red, or brown iron deposits in the chalk cliffs. When examined under a microscope, small beads and elliptic discs are visible, between them shells of prehistoric marine life and coral remnants. The diversity of forms stemming from the calcareous shells of the marine life of the Cretaceous period creates an idiosyncratic, soft surface quality that responds extra- ordinarily to light. Chalk is only opaque when used in distemper paints. When using other binders, its unique color may be approximated by adding umber to a matt white paint.

CMYK approximation:
0.5.20.0

RGB approximation:
251.243.213

Spatial qualities:
passive and stable under
all light conditions

Historical pigmentation:
lead white (in oil) or chalk
and ocher (in glue)

Industrial pigmentation:
titanium white with ocher and
umber

Facade suitability:
weather-resistant

32.001

Cream / Crème

A shade of Le Corbusier's color palette from 1931[5]

Le Corbusier's architecture is characterized by a clever interplay of light/dark and structure/empty space contrasts.[6] The light-reflecting white background was understood to be of central importance in this interplay in the purist architecture of the 1920s. The strongly shaded white of the color Cream is very close to the interior and exterior white of the Villa La Roche in Paris (Le Corbusier, Pierre Jeanneret). "All in white, the house is like a pot of cream,"[7] wrote Le Corbusier in 1926, and with that he is pointing out that his white had the color of cream, and not the color of milk or porcelain, for instance. This building, now the headquarters of the Fondation Le Corbusier, is a masterful example of how color can be used against a lively, white background that is not overly glaring, to emphasize the three-dimensional aspects of a space. The color of the lead white and chalk pigments used in this architecture may be recreated with a balanced mixture of natural umber and warm ocher. This balance lends Cream an aesthetic stability for interior or exterior surfaces.

5 Le Corbusier, *Claviers de Couleurs Salubra*, (Basel, 1931).
See also Arthur Rüegg (ed.), *Polychromie architecturale. Le Corbusiers Farbenklaviaturen von 1931 und 1959/ Le Corbusier's Color Keyboards from 1931 and 1959/ Les claviers de couleurs de Le Corbusier de 1931 et de 1959* (Basel, Boston, Berlin, 1997) (reprint, 2006).
6 Kenneth Frampton, *Modern Architecture. A Critical History* (London, [4]2007), p. 149.
7 Le Corbusier, *Almanach de l'Architecture moderne* (Paris, 1926).

CMYK approximation:
2.2.5.0

RGB approximation:
250.249.243

Spatial qualities:
passive and stable under
all light conditions

Historical pigmentation:
marble dust in glue binder

Industrial pigmentation:
marble dust with very little
titanium white

Facade suitability:
weather-resistant

32.002

Marble white / Blanc marbre

A lighter version of 43.2 Ivoire, 2002

The word marble originates from the ancient Greek *marmaros*, which means to shimmer
or to shine. Chalk and marble are both calcium carbonates, but marble is a meta-
morphic rock, not a precipitate. Marble is created when heat and pressure encounter
limestone in the earth's interior. Motion of the earth's crust and flowing water carrying
admixtures of iron (red and brown), graphite (gray), limonite (yellow), or serpentine
(green) give the stone its marbled structure. There are no fossils in marble; a distinctive
characteristic is the glimmering of individual calcite crystals in the cleavage planes
of the stone. Ground or sifted marble, which is the basis of this pigment, is characterized by its shimmering transparency. The color hue of Marble white is somewhere
between 32.000 White light and 43.2 Ivoire, which makes it a luminous and shimmering,
only slightly off-white color.

CMYK approximation:
0.2.11.0

RGB approximation:
254.250.233

Spatial qualities:
passive and stable under
all light conditions

Historical pigmentation:
travertine

Industrial pigmentation:
titanium white tinted with
umber and ocher

Facade suitability:
weather-resistant

32.003

Travertine / Blanc travertin

Reference: a stone from the Getty Center facade, Los Angeles

In addition to chalk and marble, travertine is also a natural calcium carbonate stone. It is produced when lime precipitates from deposits of limestone or marble in the direct vicinity of sweet water sources to form rock deposits. Sediments of reddish hematite and yellowish limonite give it a warm, characteristically brown tint. Small plants enclosed within the rock eventually create hollow spaces shaped like the particular plant or plant part. Travertine is a product of the most recent geological age, originating less than 2.6 million years ago. The original sample used for the color here is a stone from the Getty Center in Los Angeles. The museum, designed by Richard Meier, has a glimmering facade of travertine.

CMYK approximation:
0.0.5.1

RGB approximation:
253.252.243

Spatial qualities:
passive and stable under
all light conditions

Historical pigmentation:
china clay with ocher,
red ocher, green umber,
ultramarine blue

Industrial pigmentation:
titanium white tinted with
spinel pigments

Facade suitability:
weather-resistant

32.004

Silver white / Blanc argenté

A color of the Baumann Prase color card of 1912 [8]

A complete spectrum of colors can be produced using ocher, red ocher, green
umber, and ultramarine blue, but it is a very muted one. Adding this pale rainbow of
natural earth tones to a white color creates a silvery, shimmering white with a beautiful
play of light. Silver white could be defined as the endpoint of a cool series of grays
also including 43.19 Gris foncé, 43.8 Gris moyen, and 43.14 Gris clair. Combined
with ultramarine blue tones, this series of cool grays takes on a cold, metallic quality.
Combinations with other colors are lively in the changing daylight. The delicate
color particles in Silver white emerge and whisper softly to light, to other colors, and
to ambient materials. This impression of a whisper arises if the whole spectrum of
colors is represented in a hue, but none of them dominates.

8 Otto Prase, *Baumanns Neue Farbtonkarte System Prase*
(Aue / Saxony, 1912).

CMYK approximation:
0.0.9.0

RGB approximation:
255.253.239

Spatial qualities:
passive and stable under
all light conditions

Historical pigmentation:
alabaster powder

Industrial pigmentation:
titanium white tinted with
yellow oxide and umber

Facade suitability:
weather-resistant

32.005

Alabaster white / Blanc albâtre

A color of the Baumann Prase color card of 1912[9]

Alabaster is a widespread, monoclinic crystallized gypsum. It is transparent to translucent, and can, according to where it has been mined, range in color from gentle ocher to gray. The shimmering quality of natural alabaster can be reproduced by adding balanced amounts of ocher and umber to titanium white, along with transparent fillers such as calcite, marble powder, and kaolin. This creates a carefree, elegant white with the lightness of the ocher and the shadowy qualities of umber. 43.2 Ivoire from Le Corbusier's color scale contains more umber and is hence more grayed. Both nuances manage to appear neither too sweetly yellow, stuffy and old-fashioned, nor flat and lifeless when applied to a surface, as is often the case with modern white nuances that are created with simpler mixtures. 32.005 Alabaster is a natural white that is pleasant, cheerful, and warm.

9 Prase, 1912.

CMYK approximation:
0.1.2.3

RGB approximation:
248.246.244

Spatial qualities:
passive and stable under
all light conditions,
especially effective in the
shade

Historical pigmentation:
shale with chalk

Industrial pigmentation:
titanium white tinted
with chrome green,
red oxide, and yellow oxide

Facade suitability:
weather-resistant

32.006

Shale white / Blanc ardoise

A traditional white distemper paint until circa 1950

Argillaceous shale was mined mainly in the Rhine River and in the Eifel region
of Germany. The hardness and the gentle gray hue of the shale, which is also called
silver gray, mineral gray, or stone gray, makes it a popular pigment for cement and
artificial stone. Although argillaceous shale is less abundant than chalk, its distinctive,
warm gray hue has made it a favorite supplementary pigment for shimmering gray
distemper paints. It dries hard and brittle. The mixture of soft, creamy chalks
with ground, stone gray argillaceous shale creates a subtle, warm, and shadowy
white called Shale white.

CMYK approximation:
0.2.3.6

RGB approximation:
242.239.235

Spatial qualities:
passive and stable under
all light conditions,
especially effective in
the shade

Historical pigmentation:
shale with chalk

Industrial pigmentation:
titanium white tinted
with chrome green, red
oxide, and yellow oxide

Facade suitability:
weather-resistant

32.007

Rosa Caso's gray / Gris Caso

A lighter version of the color 32.013 Gris perle

Gris caso was created for an interior designer named Rosa Caso who was looking
for a luminous gray between 32.004 Silver white und 32.013 Gris perle. Due to its gray
content, Gris caso is an excellent white for rooms that have little daylight. It is an
elegant gray in sunny spaces, and very pleasant in dark spaces. Pure white and other
bright colors are less appropriate for spaces with little light, because they emphasize
the lack of windows and other shortcomings. The best colors for darker spaces are
those that boast a sense of discretion. A fair half-shadow allows embarrassing aspects
to be hidden. Other colors that possess this ability are 32.014 Gris natur, 32.143
Terre d'ombre naturelle pâle, and 08.013 Terre d'ombre brûlée pâle.

CMYK approximation:
0.0.0.0

RGB approximation:
255.255.255

Spatial qualities:
passive and stable under
all light conditions

Historical pigmentation:
burnt kaolin

Industrial pigmentation:
titanium white with baked clay
circa 1:2

Facade suitability:
weather-resistant

32.009

China clay white / Blanc porcelaine

A traditional pure white until circa 1930

Kaolin (Chinese for "high chain of mountains") is a silicate aluminum compound; it is also called china clay, potter's clay, porcelain earth, and, in old books of painting, silicate white. Locations with the finest clays, for example in Dresden and Meißen in Germany, the region of Bohemia in today's Czech Republic, Copenhagen, or Spode in England, were made world-famous by the porcelain manufacturers in those areas. Kaolin is mainly a raw material for use in ceramic production, but porcelain earth is also used to make ultramarine and can be used as a transparent, color-pure white pigment. The kaolin content in the color China clay white can be made more opaque by adding titanium white in proportionate amounts of circa two parts kaolin to one part titanium white. The clarity and purity of the shade, which comes from the kaolin content, remains intact.

CMYK approximation:
0.2.7.5

RGB approximation:
244.240.230

Spatial qualities:
passive and stable under
all light conditions

Historical pigmentation:
chalk tinted with umber

Industrial pigmentation:
titanium white tinted with
chrome green, red oxide,
and yellow oxide

Facade suitability:
weather-resistant

32.014

Natural gray / Gris natur

A traditional white distemper paint until circa 1950 and a classic mixing white

This white color originated as an additional lighter hue in the series of colors made with raw umber, ending with 32.143 Terre d'ombre naturelle pâle. Gris natur is based on the same pigmentation as all the colors in this series. Natural pigments lend this velvety off-white color tinged with a brownish-gray umber its soft quality, which is calm and muted. A splendid color chart, most likely from a German prewar paint factory, since color chart production was then still a respected craft, shows twenty-three saturated full tone colors, from each of which twenty-seven light and dark shades are derived. This white produced all of the charming pastels. Not one looks flat, artificial or sweet, which is a remarkable achievement made possible by using this balanced white. By the same token, Gris natur is an integrative background color that ties everything in a room together, rejecting nothing.

CMYK approximation:
3.0.6.0

RGB approximation:
249.251.243

Spatial qualities:
passive and stable under
all light conditions,
especially effective in the
shade

Historical pigmentation:
zinc oxide red seal

Industrial pigmentation:
titanium white tinted
with ultramarine blue and
umber

Facade suitability:
weather-resistant

32.025

Glacial white / Glacier

A traditional white distemper paint until circa 1950

At the beginning of the twentieth century, two white pigments dominated artistic assortments: warm lead white and cold zinc white. Painters knew how to mute and darken colors by adding the complement, and they also knew that zinc white could lighten ultramarine and Prussian blue to create the most beautiful derivatives. In contrast, lead white could lighten other colors such as scarlet red, turning them into beautiful pastel shades. As a distemper paint, without any other additional color content, zinc white is called Glacial white. The ambition to reduce the negative effects on the environment by reducing metallic chelating agents such as zinc, led to a new zinc-free formulation of the cool shade. It only requires traces of an umber and ultramarine blue mixture in order to arrive at this idiosyncratic, airy color that is also very effective in the shade.

CMYK approximation:
5.0.5.0

RGB approximation:
246.249.244

Spatial qualities:
passive and stable under
all light conditions

Historical pigmentation:
China clay white with
malachite crystals,
not suitable for facades

Industrial pigmentation:
titanium white with
cobalt green, suitable
for facades

32.049

Malachite white / Blanc malachite

China clay white tinted with malachite, 2001

Malachite is quite common among the minerals of the carbonate group. Together
with azurite, it belongs to the cupreous minerals of this crystal system. Malachite is
characterized by its green color, which exhibits strong pleochroism and a variable
color ranging from yellow-green to deep green. Pleochroism means that there is a visible
change in color when viewed under light polarized in different directions. Under the
microscope, the historically pigmented version of Malachite white displays small
rock crystals that create a sparkling greenish white that appears ghostly in the shade.
Even if Malachite white is tinted with industrial pigments, it has a crystal clear hue,
which means that it is the coolest shade in this chapter of whites.

CMYK approximation:
5.0.1.0

RGB approximation:
246.250.251

Spatial qualities:
passive and stable under
all light conditions,
especially effective in the
shade

Historical pigmentation:
china clay with lapis lazuli
3 %, not suitable for facades

Industrial pigmentation:
titanium white with
ultramarine blue, suitable
for facades

32.029

Lapis lazuli white / Blanc lapis-lazuli

China clay white tinted with lapis lazuli, 2001

Lapis means stone in Latin, and lazuli comes from the Arabic word *lazulum*, which means "blue." Hence, lapis lazuli simply means blue stone. The famous semi-precious stone, an intimate mixture of the minerals lasurite, pyrite, and calcite, can be found in volcanic deposits in Afghanistan, Chile, Russia, and California. The blue color is unique because it is intensely luminous when used in chapels and other dark spaces. Particles of sulfur radicals inside the crystals absorb invisible light waves and transform them into blue color, an ability that only lapis lazuli and its industrially manufactured sister, ultramarine blue, can boast. Adding to white about three percent of the semi-precious stone or a trace of synthetic ultramarine blue lends it an indescribably cool, luminous quality, and a heavenly effect that transcends description.

CMYK approximation:
0.2.1.0

RGB approximation:
254.251.250

Spatial qualities:
passive and stable under
all light conditions

Historical pigmentation:
kaolin with burnt Sienna

Industrial pigmentation:
titanium white with iron
oxide pigment

Facade suitability:
weather-resistant

32.124

White with burnt Sienna / Blanc de terre de Sienne

A color of the Baumann Prase color card of 1912 [10]

Dark to brownish-black wooden floors of mahogany or walnut are most handsome
when they border white walls painted with muted, almost imperceptible orange or red
hues such as those created by adding burnt Sienna or burnt umber to a matt white.
Even a small added amount of the warm, brownish-red earth from the Siena region
provides a basic white with color and texture. If natural earth is used to give an apricot
hue to a white color, the white will always have a very earthy and not overly sweet
quality. In general, such pigments do more than just tint another color, they may also
convey earthy qualities (if they contain large crystals of natural earths), airy
qualities (ultramarines), watery qualities (transparent pigments in all color areas), or
metallic qualities (through synthetically produced iron oxide pigments), to name
just a few.

10 Prase, 1912.

CMYK approximation:
0.4.2.0

RGB approximation:
253.248.246

Spatial qualities:
passive and stable under
all light conditions

Historical pigmentation:
lime or chalk with
burnt umber

Industrial pigmentation:
titanium white with iron
oxide pigment

Facade suitability:
weather-resistant

32.132

White with burnt umber / Blanc d'ombre brûlé

A color of the Baumann Prase color card of 1912 [11]

Traces of mahogany brown-colored burnt umber generate white colors with a
gentle reddish hue similar to the touch of pink found inside some white blossoms. Such
a pink's light, luminous quality differs greatly from the dyed-looking synthetic pinks
made from artificial pigments, because the latter do not remind us of anything natural.
Lafcadio Hearn described natural pink in context with the Japanese cherry blossoms
as a soft roseate: "the most ethereal pink, a flushed white. When in spring the
trees flower, it is as though fleeciest masses of cloud faintly touched with sunset had
floated down from the highest sky to fold themselves about the branches. This
comparison is no poetic exaggeration [...]" [12] The beauty of this tinted white unfolds
to its most beautiful with dark wooden floor boards or mahogany brown parquet.

11 Prase, 1912.
12 Lafcadio Hearn, "In a Japanese Garden," in *Glimpses of an Unfamiliar Japan: Second Series* (Teddington, 2006) p. 9.

CMYK approximation:
0.0.10.0

RGB approximation:
255.253.236

Spatial qualities:
passive and stable under
all light conditions

Historical pigmentation:
lime, chalk, or lead white,
according to binder

Industrial pigmentation:
titanium white with red or
green umber

Facade suitability:
weather-resistant

43.2

Ivory / Ivoire

A shade of Le Corbusier's color palette from 1931[13] and 1959[14]

This was the epitomic white of early modernism. The color is similar to that of elephant tusks. It is a hushed alternative to the rather loud and bright industrial white colors, such as RAL 9010 or NCS S 0500, and it can be compared to the beautiful color of lead white in poppy oil, or that of a simple whitewashed facade, or the charming light color of some chalks less pure and expensive than Bologna white, but somewhat purer than Champagne white. The paint industry's rationalization process replaced this gentle, light-reflective background color in favor of the light-scattering, more opaque whites made from barium sulfate or lithopone and later from titanium white. The beauty of the color Ivoire lies in its balance and discretion, and makes it a perfect atmospheric background color for the white rooms of all architectural eras.

13 Le Corbusier, 1931; Rüegg, 1997 (reprint, 2006).
14 Le Corbusier, 1959; Rüegg, 1997 (reprint, 2006).

The Grays and Blacks

Since the evaluation of some colors is often metaphorically connected to light, and gray was not originally considered a color, it frequently carries a negative connotation.[6] Gray has been neglected by the field of architecture, due, at least in part, to the two different interpretations of the concept of "gray." Slate, sand stone, granite, eroded wood, volcanic stone, gneiss, feldspar, graphite are all gray, which implies that the first logical meaning of gray describes a color of objects. The second describes a transparent, symbolically loaded gray: the gray of fog, a gloomy mood, sorrow, or storm clouds. Gray results from phenomena that signify a real or felt lack of light. However, gray, as the color of an object, should never be confused with gray as a quality of light. A gray wall is *visible*, and the gray of its walls will place it in shadow. A landscape is *invisible* through a cloud of mist. A visible gray wall is not suggestive of fog or mist,[7] but rather a surface that is not fully lit and somewhat receding.

If the many gradations of the white-to-black, light-to-dark scale remain tethered to symbolic, light- and color-related associations, there is the risk of conveying these preconceptions to architecture. One consequence of this would be, for instance, to paint everything white, and thus disregard the three-dimensional differentiation that can be achieved by a strategic use of gradations of gray.

"Rolf Schön: Why do you repudiate colour?
Gerhard Richter: Grey is a colour – and sometimes, to me, the most important colour."
Gerhard Richter [1]

"Shadow, said Augustine, is the Queen of Colour. Colour sings in the grey. Painters often have grey studio walls, for instance the grey-papered walls on which Géricault hung his paintings.
Grey makes a perfect background. The walls of Matisse's studio were grey [...]."
Derek Jarman [2]

Skillful color design with gray follows the principles of black and white photography. Anything gray will look as if it is only partially lit. If the gray is lighter in color, it will look more illuminated and will seem closer. The darker it is, the less illuminated and farther away it will seem. Three-dimensional depth is achieved by gradations of contrast. In other words, whatever is lighter in color will be more visible in a room and will have a stronger presence. The darker the color, the more an object will withdraw into the background and distract attention from itself by receding into the shadows. Consequently, grays can control the amount of attention a surface or an object is given. If an area is to be shown, it can be white or light gray, if it is to be hidden, it should be painted with darker gray

tones. Gray is a better color for low ceilings than white, because a white ceiling is perceived as being more evident. White will emphasize, gray will conceal.
In nature, not only clouds and fog are gray, but also stones, metals, and weathered wood. The colors of the gray scale range from warm and yellowish to cool and bluish, and from almost white to almost black. The surface appearance ranges from soft and velvety to hard and metallic, and the density from light and fleeting to heavy and insistent. Light, warm, and matt grays are more gentle, lighter and warmer. Increasing the black and blue content, or the gloss, makes grays cooler, more solid, and metallic. Most grays are created from tinted black-white mixtures. However, a more beautiful effect can be achieved by mixing gray from the complementary colors, such as red and green (just as it is better to mute or darken bright colors with complementary colors, for instance by adding chrome green or umber to Pompeian red). In gray mixtures, the white pigment, being weaker in tinting strength than dark pigments, almost always predominates in quantity, and grays with a textural color feel are made using beautiful white pigments.

Mixtures of umber and white were among the important groups of shadowy gray paints before industrialization. The exquisitely beautiful gray umbers are so important that the next chapter is dedicated to them alone. Here, we will examine the less colorful and cooler shades of gray, as well as black and Prussian blue.

Prussian blue and black, both at the end of the light-to-dark array of colors, are both unique. Glossy black surfaces reflect light and surrounding colors. Their surfaces function as mirrors. They differ from matt black surfaces that absorb light and contrast strongly with the surrounding colors. Prussian blue is almost a black and behaves similarly. Regardless of how glossy they are, black and Prussian blue can have a dramatic and mysterious effect. Used deliberately, they can be potent members of the colorists' design palette.

1 Gerhard Richter, *The Daily Practice of Painting. Writings and Interviews 1962–1993* (London, 1995), p. 75.
2 Derek Jarman, *Chroma. A Book of Colour* (London, 1994), p. 51.
3 Translated from Ludwig Wittgenstein, *Bemerkungen über die Farben* (Frankfurt, 1977), p. 78.
4 Translated from Ingrid Riedel, *Farben in Religion, Gesellschaft, Kunst und Psychotherapie* (Stuttgart, 1999), p. 190.
5 Translated from Harald Haarmann, *Schwarz. Eine kleine Kulturgeschichte* (Frankfurt, 2005), p. 35.
6 This is similar to the color black, see Beate Epperlein, *Monochrome Malerei* (Nuremberg, 1997) p. 97.
7 Ludwig Wittgenstein examined this logical and theoretical contradiction. White wine and milk should not both be described using the logical term "white." See note 3.

CMYK approximation:
60.25.0.90

RGB approximation:
22.27.34

Spatial qualities:
dynamic and stable under
all light conditions

Historical pigmentation:
Prussian blue

Industrial pigmentation:
phthalocyanine blue with
carbon black

Facade suitability:
not weather-resistant

04.003

Prussian blue / Bleu de Prusse

On every color palette until the advent of acrylic binders

This wonderful pigment was discovered at a time when discoveries and inventions often happened by chance. In 1704 in Berlin, a color chemist named Diesbach was experimenting with fluids that he had mixed using a familiar recipe. However, he did not get the carmine red color he was expecting. Instead, an unknown, beautiful blue color emerged from the mixture. The color was so beautiful that he decided to research its basis. He discovered that the inexpensive potash he was using contained traces of potassium ferrocyanide from the calcination of potash with blood. He was astonished to discover that adding a solution of iron salts to the reaction vial resulted in the exquisite color of Prussian blue.[8] Its brilliance makes it an excellent translucent color in all techniques and irreplaceable as an oil paint for artists.

8 Erich Stock, *Die Grundlagen des Lack- und Farbenfachs*, volume IV
  (Meißen, 1924), p. 99–100.

CMYK approximation:
40.0.0.100

RGB approximation:
0.0.0

Spatial qualities:
dynamic and stable under
all light conditions

Historical pigmentation:
bone black (ivory black)

Industrial pigmentation:
carbon black

Facade suitability:
weather-resistant

43.5

Ivory black / Noir

A shade of Le Corbusier's color palette from 1959 [9]

Charred blacks derived from animal, vegetable, and mineral sources are ancient colorants. Animal-based blacks are produced from bones, and vegetable-based blacks from different types of vegetable waste such as pomace, wine yeasts, vines, molasses, fruit stones and pits, nutshells, coffee grounds, chestnuts, cork waste, oil cake, tanbark, hops residue, and bark. Le Corbusier used noir ivoire or "ivory black," which is a romantic term for the best quality of the black made by charring bones. Ivory black is composed of a mixture of charred bones and charcoal. Its opacity and intense depth of color are astonishing. The dictionary specifies that the end of the black spectrum, an absolute black, is technically not possible. The ivory black pigment in glue-based techniques, however, yields a depth of color close to absolute black and unattainable with carbon black or black iron oxide.

9 Le Corbusier, *Claviers de Couleurs Salubra 2* (Basel, 1959).
   See also Arthur Rüegg (ed.), *Polychromie architecturale. Le Corbusiers Farbenklaviaturen von 1931 und 1959 / Le Corbusier's Color Keyboards from 1931 and 1959 / Les claviers de couleurs de Le Corbusier de 1931 et de 1959* (Basel, Boston, Berlin, 1997) (reprint, 2006).

CMYK approximation:
30.0.0.90

RGB approximation:
33.37.40

Spatial qualities:
dynamic and stable under
all light conditions

Historical pigmentation:
ivory black and Champagne
white, 1:1

Industrial pigmentation:
black oxide, titanium white,
and yellow oxide

Facade suitability:
weather-resistant

10.010

Anthracite / Anthracite

The Second Gradation of the Ostwald Gray Scale, 1912[10]

A perfect gray scale ranging from 43.5 Noir to 32.013 Gris perle can be created.
With 32.014 Gris natur and 08.001 Champagne white, which are both classified under
the whites, an eight-step, light-to-dark scale can be generated. Such a gray scale
of non-neutral grays was central to all traditional color systems. Anthracite is the first
gradation after black, and is surprisingly made from equal measures of ivory black
and Champagne white, because white pigments are much less intense than black pigments. The chemist and Nobel Prize winner Wilhelm Ostwald recognized that
uniform gradations of gray values are created when the white content is doubled from
gradation to gradation. This creates a perfect gray scale that ranges from dark
to light, using the following mixtures of Noir and Champagne white: pure 43.5 Noir,
$\frac{1}{1}$, $\frac{1}{2}$, $\frac{1}{4}$, $\frac{1}{8}$, $\frac{1}{16}$, $\frac{1}{32}$, pure 08.001 Champagne white.

10 Wilhelm Ostwald, *Einführung in die Farbenlehre*, Reclam Bücher der Naturwissenschaft
    (Leipzig, 1919).

CMYK approximation:
5.0.0.70

RGB approximation:
96.97.99

Spatial qualities:
dynamic and stable under
all light conditions

Historical pigmentation:
ivory black and Champagne
white

Industrial pigmentation:
black oxide, titanium
white, and yellow oxide

Facade suitability:
weather-resistant

32.010

Ferric gray / Gris fer

A shade of Le Corbusier's color palette from 1931 [11]

Le Corbusier managed to contain the foreignness of his modern architecture by gracing its elements with familiar, discrete color values borrowed from nature. This placed the strange, new architecture in a more gentle light. The color palette used for the white architecture of the 1920s, conceived according to the strict principles of the purist era, consists of fourteen saturated color nuances with numerous gradations. The mild, warm color 32.010 Gris fer replaces black as the darkest nuance of the purist gray scale. The subtle colors of the purist palette created poetic backgrounds in Le Corbusier's architecture. The entire purist gray scale, running from shadowed to luminous, contains: 32.010 Gris fer, 32.011 Gris, 32.012 Gris clair 2, 32.013 Gris perle, 32.001 Crème. Gris fer was often used as an oil paint for radiators and other metal parts.

---

11 Le Corbusier, *Claviers de Couleurs Salubra* (Basel, 1931).
    See also Arthur Rüegg (ed.), *Polychromie architecturale. Le Corbusiers Farbenklaviaturen von 1931 und 1959 / Le Corbusier's Color Keyboards from 1931 and 1959 / Les claviers de couleurs de Le Corbusier de 1931 et de 1959* (Basel, Boston, Berlin, 1997) (reprint, 2006).

CMYK approximation:
0.0.0.55

RGB approximation:
136.136.136

Spatial qualities:
dynamic and stable under
all light conditions

Historical pigmentation:
ivory black and Champagne
white

Industrial pigmentation:
black oxide, titanium white,
and yellow oxide

Facade suitability:
weather-resistant

32.011

Gray / Gris

A shade of Le Corbusier's color palette from 1931 [12]

32.011 Gris is located in the center of Le Corbusier's light-to-dark scale of gray
tonalities that gradually become lighter and more luminous. Gris is an elegant, discrete
nuance active across the entire visible spectrum of colors. It is created from one
part ivory black and four parts Champagne white (lead white was used in earlier oil
paint production). Mixing velvety ivory black pigment and Champagne white, a
product of lime seashell deposits, produces a lively effect and a characteristic velvety
texture. Wittgenstein wrote, "if something looks luminous, it will not look gray," [13]
thereby providing instructions for how to use color mixtures such as these. These
darker nuances will make surfaces recede as if in shadow. Lighter-colored objects or
surfaces placed nearby will seem more luminous when situated against a backdrop
such as this.

12 Ibid.
13 Wittgenstein (1977), p. 18.

CMYK approximation:
0.0.0.40

RGB approximation:
170.170.170

Spatial qualities:
dynamic and stable under
all light conditions

Historical pigmentation:
ivory black and Champagne
white

Industrial pigmentation:
black oxide, titanium white,
and yellow oxide

Facade suitability:
weather-resistant

32.012

Light gray 2 / Gris clair 2

A shade of Le Corbusier's color palette from 1931 [14]

Gris clair 2 corresponds roughly to the color of a shadow on a white background on a sunny mid-afternoon. The eye will seek relief from too much glaring white by retreating and resting in the shadows. In a society that often equates quality with quantity, creating spaces in which every nook and cranny is brightly lit has become almost rule of thumb. Since white colors leave more light energy in the room, thus the reasoning, one can save energy by avoiding colors, which are known to absorb light. This, however, completely ignores the fact that a feeling of well-being does not necessarily go together with imposed brightness. Gentle, shady colors such as gris clair impart a discrete quietude to a room that does not need to be banished by light. Quietude is a pleasure.

14 Le Corbusier, 1931; Rüegg, 1997 (reprint, 2006).

CMYK approximation:
0.0.5.30
RGB approximation:
192.191.185

Spatial qualities:
static, constructive,
beautiful in shade

Historical pigmentation:
ivory black and Champagne
white

Industrial pigmentation:
titanium white with
green umber and tinted with
red oxide

Facade suitability:
weather-resistant

32.013

Pearl gray / Gris perle

A shade of Le Corbusier's color palette from 1931[15]

During the peak of Le Corbusier's purist architectural designs based on principles
of harmony and order, he wrote that if a color is supposed to fuse with but not dominate
the architecture, then one should use a limited palette of gentle, natural colors.[16]
Light gray colors such as Gris perle play an essential role in this series of constructive
colors, because gray actually conducts light. The graduated gray scale that ranges
from nuances 10.010 Gris fer to 32.013 Gris perle serves to conduct light, rather
than add coloration. "Anything gray looks illuminated. A thing can be seen as weakly
lit or as gray," wrote Wittgenstein.[17] White colors visibly bring surfaces to the fore,
shimmering gray values such as this look dimly lit, and dark grays place surfaces
in shadow.

15 Ibid.
16 Charles-Edouard Jeanneret (Le Corbusier) and Amédée Ozenfant,
   "Le Purisme," in *L'Esprit Nouveau* 4, 1921.
17 Wittgenstein, 1977, p. 18–19

CMYK approximation:
25.10.0.70

RGB approximation:
80.83.91

Spatial qualities:
dynamic and stable under
all light conditions

Historical pigmentation:
unclear, different possibilities

Industrial pigmentation:
black oxide and titanium
white with inorganic color
pigments

Facade suitability:
weather-resistant

43.19

Deep gray / Gris foncé

A shade of Le Corbusier's color palette from 1959[18]

Le Corbusier's architecture after 1950 was characterized by the interplay of different materials such as natural stone, wood, concrete, brick, and glass. After breaking with the tradition of white forms in his purist architecture, he began working with a new, more powerful color palette with a reduced number of nuances. The warm gray scale with four gradations from the purist era now turns into a cool gray scale consisting of 43.19 Gris foncé, 43.8 Gris moyen, and 43.14 Gris clair. The color displayed here looks very metallic; it replaces the warm, soft purist dark gray, 32.010 Gris fer. The cool gray color is particularly beautiful when used as a satin varnish for furniture or structural components, and forms a convincing contrast to 43.20 Jaune vif and the other deep, saturated colors in Le Corbusier's 1959 collection.

18 Le Corbusier, 1959; Rüegg, 1997 (reprint, 2006).

CMYK approximation:
15.0.0.60

RGB approximation:
110.116.121

Spatial qualities:
dynamic and stable under
all light conditions

Historical pigmentation:
unclear, different possibilities

Industrial pigmentation:
black oxide and titanium
white with inorganic color
pigments

Facade suitability:
weather-resistant

43.8

Medium gray / Gris moyen

A shade of Le Corbusier's color palette from 1959[19]

The second nuance in Le Corbusier's cool gray series serves as a highly effective contrast to the deep ultramarine and umber nuances of the 1959 color scale. The gray values of the 1920s scale made with umber increased the plasticity of white spaces, the metallic grays of the 1950s were more prominent and dynamic because the bymixed colors were made with dense pigments, such as cobalt blue. It is interesting to note that Le Corbusier combined natural concrete surfaces with strong nuances made from synthetic pigments in the 1950s, and combined white surfaces with more muted nuances mostly made from natural pigments in the 1920s. Saturated colors are more effective with naturally colored materials and large dimensions than with white walls and small spaces, where they become too dominant.

19 Ibid.

CMYK approximation:
10.0.0.40

RGB approximation:
158.164.168

Spatial qualities:
dynamic and stable under
all light conditions

Historical pigmentation:
unclear, different possibilities

Industrial pigmentation:
black oxide and titanium
white with inorganic color
pigments

Facade suitability:
weather-resistant

43.14

Light gray / Gris clair

A shade of Le Corbusier's color palette from 1959 [20]

The lightest nuance in Le Corbusier's 1959 gray series shimmers as cool as the morning's dawn. It is a color that makes objects and surfaces look veiled. The whole gray series, which is characterized by its slight blue-violet hue, can be compared to the ghostly appearance of the Blueridge Mountains at dawn, or other mountains, which are already visible, but not yet bathed in sunlight. Cennini wrote in the Middle Ages [21] that when drawing a mountain "the farther away you have to make the mountains look, the darker you make your colors; and the nearer you are making them seem, the lighter you make the colors." Gris clair recedes when placed against a white background, against a darker color, such as 43.19 Gris foncé, it will advance.

20 Ibid.
21 Cennino d'Andrea Cennini, *The Craftman's Handbook "Il Libro dell'Arte,"* (Dover, New York, 1960), p. 55–56.

CMYK approximation:
30.7.0.40

RGB approximation:
131.143.159

Spatial qualities:
dynamic and stable under
all light conditions

Historical pigmentation:
azurite with white

Industrial pigmentation:
cobalt blue with red oxide
and titanium white

Facade suitability:
weather-resistant

20-30.5

Natier blue / Bleu Natier

A color from the Plastor company color card, found in Le Corbusier's estate, 1920–1930[22]

Bleu Natier is a unique case among the blues. It is classified with the grays, rather than the blues, due to its discrete, metallic, blue-gray quality. Bleu Natier is not an ideal color for ceilings, because it is too heavy. Yet it can be used to confirm the presence of a wall, unlike blue paints made with ultramarine blue, which have a receding effect. This shade is based on an original sample from a color chart of a now defunct, color-manufacturing company called Plastor that was found among Le Corbusier's estate. Jean-Marc Natier (1642–1705), a well-known French portrait painter, used such a color to portray the heavy, velvet robes of royalty. Le Corbusier, following a similar idea, used this optically stable blue to varnish the oval feet of the prototypes of his early chaise lounges.

22 Color card of the Plastor company, archives of the Fondation Le Corbusier,
dated between 1920 and 1930.

The Umbers

The last chapter explained that gray paints conduct light rather than impart color: light shades illuminate objects or surfaces; dark ones will place them in shadow. Conversely, gray surfaces in shady spaces are uniquely effective, because their ability to balance the lack of light renders them ideal for dark rooms.

These ideas apply to the umbers in particular. These pigments were produced when the ocean floor swept over the landmass, which created mountain chains with local deposits of umber. The striking attributes of porous umbers originate from their geological composition, which includes silicon compounds, manganite, pyrolusite, and goethite—in other words, colorless crystals, black grains, dark gray shiny pellets, and yellow-to-red iron compounds. It is easy to imagine how beautiful it is when even modest amounts of light encounter colorful or sparkling substances, triggering an interplay of color and light. The best quality of umbers from Cyprus are warm and dark with a brownish-violet hue that can become a deeper, redder, magnificent Chestnut brown by means of calcination, a process that eliminates their crystal water.

In spite of the fact that the Ajanta cave paintings, dated at circa 200 BC, used umber pigments, these pigments had to wait until the Middle Ages and the invention of perspectival painting before they would become a standard component of any painter's palette. Mixtures using white created a warm, yellowish-brown shade that quickly established itself as a shadow color for fine art and surface painters. The effect of umber as a shadow color is fourfold:

- It creates exquisite shadow effects in paintings.
- Bright colors can be muted without flattening their color reflexes.
- Painted surfaces and volumes are discrete and withdraw into shadow.
- Ceilings and walls that are already shadowed work so well with umbers that the lack of light will not be noticed.
- The variable, multi-colored composition of umbers allows for something else. Since they contain almost every other color, they will harmonize and complement nearly any surrounding color. Raw umbers, neither reddish nor greenish in hue, wonderfully regulate or balance anything nearby that is too colorful, be it the contents of a room or bright paintings on a wall.

Today, umbers are made mostly from iron oxide yellow and iron oxide black. If no other pigments are added to the mixture, the characteristic green, red, or violet content

"Shadow is the proper element of color, and in this case a subdued color approaches it lighting up, tinging, and enlivening it. And thus arises an appearance, as powerful as agreeable, which may render the most pleasing service to a painter who knows how to make use of it."

Johann Wolfgang von Goethe [1]

of the raw umbers will be missing, and they will lose their ability to be true masters of transformation. Complex pigment mixtures restore it.

Dark, raw umbers can have a solid, camouflage effect — Le Corbusier's 43.16 Terre d'ombre naturelle foncée is a good example of this. Adding a small amount of white imparts the color with an elegance that endures through to the lightest color value.

Saturated, burnt umbers look natural and noble, but lighter versions of these can look fleshy and heavy. For this reason, they have to be mixed carefully. It is essential to add complementary colors in order to achieve a pleasant, natural effect. Such hues are less present in this chapter than light raw umbers, these being the hues that cannot be underestimated in their ability to create atmospheres of tranquility.

1 Johann Wolfgang von Goethe, *Theory of Colours* (London, 1840), section 591, p. 236.

CMYK approximation:
0.30.25.90

RGB approximation:
39.32.29

Spatial qualities:
dynamic, stable under all
light conditions

Historical pigmentation:
burnt umber

Industrial pigmentation:
iron oxide yellow, red, and
black, chrome green

Facade suitability:
weather-resistant

43.9

Burnt umber / Ombre brûlé

A shade of Le Corbusier's color palette from 1959[2]

This warm, dark, smoky black color from Le Corbusier's second color scale corresponds to the standard color of mahogany brown or dark maroon from the time when real, natural umber pigments dominated the market—and not the mixtures called "umber" made from artificial yellow oxide and black pigments. It is interesting to note that the 1950s palette of twenty colors contains two almost black shades plus a black. Knowing that very dark colors are perceived with more difficulty and less specificity than light colors, Le Corbusier used these mainly as camouflaging colors, so as to hide elements from which he wanted to detract attention. This black with highlights of dark red and burnt umber forms a strong contrast to the green, gray, and ultramarine shades on the color palette.

2 Le Corbusier, *Claviers de Couleurs Salubra 2* (Basel, 1959).
  See also Arthur Rüegg (ed.), *Polychromie architecturale. Le Corbusiers Farbenklaviaturen von 1931 und 1959 / Le Corbusier's Color Keyboards from 1931 and 1959 / Les claviers de couleurs de Le Corbusier de 1931 et de 1959* (Basel, Boston, Berlin, 1997) (reprint, 2006).

CMYK approximation:
0.5.10.90

RGB approximation:
41.40.38

Spatial qualities:
dynamic, stable under
all light conditions,
very beautiful in the shade

Historical pigmentation:
raw umber from Cyprus

Industrial pigmentation:
iron oxide red, chrome oxide
green, and black

Facade suitability:
weather-resistant

43.16

Native natural umber / Terre d'ombre naturelle

A shade of Le Corbusier's color palette from 1959[3]

The difference between black and a dark, grayed brown is "similar to the one between the sound of a large bass drum and the sound of a kettledrum."[4] Wittgenstein thus makes a distinction between the absoluteness of black and the mute, indecipherable quality of dark umber, a shade of brown that obliterates and conceals. "I was looking for a colour (brown cross) which was not at all experienced as a colour, which was a substance: let us say a kind of sculptural expression which was a colour, but was not a colour."[5] This quote by Joseph Beuys conveys the aesthetic expression of deep, dark umber nicely, and it precisely describes its appropriate use: the austere color of monks' robes is modest, and it serves to camouflage an object or to create a background for any color that will shine in comparison.

3 Ibid.
4 Translated from Ludwig Wittgenstein, *Bemerkungen über die Farben*
   (Frankfurt, 1977), p. 80.
5 Quoted in: *I send you this Cadmium Red… A Correspondence between John Berger and
   John Christie* (Barcelona, 2000).

CMYK approximation:
0.40.40.80

RGB approximation:
64.50.40

Spatial qualities:
dynamic, stable under all
light conditions

Historical pigmentation:
burnt umber from Cyprus

Industrial pigmentation:
iron oxide yellow, red, and
black

Facade suitability:
weather-resistant

32.130

Chestnut brown / Marron

A shade of Le Corbusier's color palette from 1931[6]

Umber from Cyprus, much appreciated by artists since the Middle Ages, is transformed into an intense shade of burnt umber when robbed of its water content by a low-temperature heating process. The opulence of this shade inspired the two descriptive nicknames of Chestnut brown and velvet brown. Such deep, brownish-red umbers are fundamentally different from other browns. They confirm the fact that the beauty as well as the durability of some traditional pigments cannot be surpassed, or in some cases even matched, by modern pigments. Artists have valued the ability of the umbers to create shadow effects to enhance the two- and three-dimensional effects in their artwork for centuries. The same capability makes them "shadow colors" for architectural purposes: umbers place surfaces in shadow, conceal their size, and diminish their presence.

6 Le Corbusier, *Claviers de Couleurs Salubra* (Basel, 1931).
See also Arthur Rüegg (ed.), *Polychromie architecturale. Le Corbusiers Farbenklaviaturen von 1931 und 1959/ Le Corbusier's Color Keyboards from 1931 and 1959 / Les claviers de couleurs de Le Corbusier de 1931 et de 1959* (Basel, Boston, Berlin, 1997) (reprint, 2006).

CMYK approximation:
20.35.40.30

RGB approximation:
149.129.111

Spatial qualities:
dynamic, stable under all
light conditions

Historical pigmentation:
burnt umber from Cyprus
with chalk white

Industrial pigmentation:
iron oxide yellow, red, and
black

Facade suitability:
weather-resistant

20-30.18

Light chestnut brown / Marron clair

A color on the Plastor company color card, found in Le Corbusier's estate, 1920–1930[7]

This lightened version of reddish-brown umber is more like clay than like a shadow. The original, like the matching blue color 20-30.5 Bleu Natier (see the chapter on "The Grays and Blacks"), can be found on a color card of the former Plastor company in Paris. Jean-Marc Natier (1642–1705), portrait painter of Louis XIV, Peter I, and Catherine I, used Bleu Natier together with this serious, fabric-like color to portray the heavy velvet of royal clothing. In contrast to the less brown and more subdued umbers, this color has a more substantial effect and will fix the plane in space. It is less suited for hiding the plane than it is for lending it the effect and the warmth and venerable character of baked clay. The original sample on the color card shows a powdery matt, glue-based paint; the pigment particles are so coarse that it is likely that the paint can be dated to the first decades of the last century. Pigments from the second half of the last century were ground more finely, which increased their color intensity, but also increased the risk of transforming their clay-like effect into an effect more reminiscent of band-aids. The complex mixture of pigments used in this color avoids that problem.

7 Color card of the Plastor company, archives of the Fondation Le Corbusier,
dated between 1920 and 1930.

CMYK approximation:
0.15.20.25

RGB approximation:
195.180.161

Spatial qualities:
passive, stable under all light conditions

Historical pigmentation:
burnt umber from Cyprus with chalk white

Industrial pigmentation:
iron oxide yellow, red, and black with titanium white

Facade suitability:
weather-resistant

32.131

Light burnt umber / Terre d'ombre brûlée claire

A shade of Le Corbusier's color palette from 1931[8]

A colorful object cannot be fully appreciated without appearing in the forefront of its own shadow. The brown background color of Victorian broaches did not emphasize the beauty of the mounted white figure, it allowed it to come into sight. Museum curators like to place marble statues against a mid-tone reddish-brown color such as this to allow the luminosity of the figures to emerge. Le Corbusier categorized this color with those that stabilize themselves in space—they neither advance nor recede— to create wonderful background effects. Terre d'ombre brûlée claire is one of the three colors assigned with the mural quality called "sand." Sand is one of the color terms in Le Corbusier's 1931 color collection used to describe a mural effect. The others are space (light ultramarine), sky (light cerulean blue), velvet (Cream and light gray), masonry (light terracotta shades), and landscape (light greens). The greatest talent this color possesses is to show white objects placed in front of or next to it to their best advantage.

8 Le Corbusier, 1931; Rüegg, 1997 (reprint, 2006).

CMYK approximation:
0.15.20.60

RGB approximation:
119.109.98

Spatial qualities:
dynamic and stable under
all light conditions,
particularly beautiful in the
shade

Historical pigmentation:
burnt umber from Cyprus with
chalk

Industrial pigmentation:
iron oxide red, yellow,
itanium white, and chrome
green

Facade suitability:
weather-resistant

08.007

Umber 272 from Cyprus / Ombra 272 Cipro

An equal mixture of 32.011 Gris and 32.141 Terre d'ombre naturelle moyenne, 2008

Evidently, it is tempting to paint a room with little daylight a friendly white, assuming that white is the best solution to the problem of darkness and that white alone can conquer the shadow. In so doing, one neglects the knowledge that artificial light can not replace natural light, and that artificial light and bright, white colors actually reveal everything, including the less attractive. White colors do not conquer the shadow, they reveal it. Another way to deal with dark rooms is to accept them, to befriend and search for beauty in the shadows. The perpetual effort to improve conditions will not calm us; peace can be found when we accept the reality. The selection of hues such as this one—and many more in this chapter—provide ideal solutions for semi-dark spaces.

CMYK approximation:
0.10.20.40

RGB approximation:
165.156.137

Spatial qualities:
passive and stable in all
light conditions,
particularly beautiful in low
light conditions

Historical pigmentation:
burnt umber from Cyprus with
chalk

Industrial pigmentation:
iron oxide red and
yellow, titanium white, and
chrome green

Facade suitability:
weather-resistant

08.006

Medium umber 272 from Cyprus / Ombra 272 Cipro media

An equal mixture of 32.012 Gris clair 2 and 32.142 Terre d'ombre naturelle claire, 2008

Similar to the previous shade of umber, the mid-range lightened version of an umber from Cyprus is somewhat less cool than Le Corbusier's gray shades, and a bit less vivid than his lightened natural umbers. Their balance and customary velvety texture make these shades an almost perfect background color for people fond of spaces that are not too glaring or brightly lit. In contrast to synthetically produced pigments, natural pigments reflect light across a wide range of wavelengths—and natural umber reflects it across the entire visible range.[9] They are consistently muted, and they adapt themselves to any situation, which makes them pleasing and integrative. These umbers prove that nature tends to be gentle on our eyes.

9 Jakob Steinbrenner and Stefan Glasauer (eds.), *Farben. Betrachtungen aus Philosophie und Naturwissenschaften* (Frankfurt, 2007), p. 279.

CMYK approximation:
0.12.20.10

RGB approximation:
227.212.188

Spatial qualities:
passive and stable in all
light conditions,
particularly beautiful in low
light conditions

Historical pigmentation:
burnt umber from Cyprus with
chalk

Industrial pigmentation:
iron oxide red, yellow,
titanium white, and chrome
green

Facade suitability:
weather-resistant

08.013

Pale native burnt umber / Terre d'ombre brûlée pâle

A lightened version of the color 32.131 Terre d'ombre brûlée claire, 2008

The heating process that transforms natural umber into burnt umber gives it a reddish hue that makes it appear more brown than gray. This is why burnt umbers have a stronger spatial presence than the natural umbers. Mid-range colors such as 20-30.18 Marron clair may appear to advance in space. Just as the shadow concept can be applied to raw umbers, mural characteristics such as sand and clay can be ascribed to the burnt umbers. This example of a gently balanced, light burnt umber looks sandy on plastered surfaces, and velvety on smooth ones. Pale, grayish-brown colors such as this one are harmonious and integrative in any context. They create an atmosphere of discretion and direct our attention to nearby colorful surfaces and objects.

CMYK approximation:
0.10.25.80

RGB approximation:
70.65.56

Spatial qualities:
dynamic and stable in all
light conditions,
particularly beautiful in low
light conditions

Historical pigmentation:
natural umber and ivory black

Industrial pigmentation:
iron oxide yellow, red, black,
and cobalt blue

Facade suitability:
weather-resistant

32.140

Deep native umber / Terre d'ombre naturelle foncée

A shade of Le Corbusier's color palette from 1931[10]

The attractiveness of these colors is emphasized in a handbook for manufacturers
of natural earth colors from 1918: "These colors are characterized by such great
beauty and depth of color that they are used for the finest paintings. Some believe the
name umber is derived from their place of origin: the province of Umbria, which is
known for its brown-colored earth. Others say it comes from the use of this mineral to
create shadows (in Latin, umber means shadow)."[11] The sheer number of shades
based on umber pigments is evidence of their importance for surfaces that are either
in shadow or should be placed in shadow. This is the darkest note of Le Corbsuier's
elegant and architecturally valuable gray-brown scale. It is a velvety brownish-
gray with deep red and green reflexes.

10 Le Corbusier, 1931; Rüegg, 1997 (reprint, 2006).
11 Josef Bersch, *Die Fabrikation der Erdfarben, Handbuch* (Vienna, Leipzig, [3]1918).

CMYK approximation:
0.10.25.50

RGB approximation:
143.135.114

Spatial qualities:
dynamic and stable in all
light conditions,
particularly beautiful in low
light conditions

Historical pigmentation:
natural umber from Cyprus

Industrial pigmentation:
iron oxide red, cobalt blue,
chrome green and black
oxide

Facade suitability:
weather-resistant

32.141

Medium native umber / Terre d'ombre naturelle moyenne

A shade of Le Corbusier's color palette from 1931 [12]

The umbers included in this chapter could be interpreted as a "rejection of the effective mechanisms of colorful colors and a disinterest in symbolic connotations." [13] Umbers are symbolically neutral because they unite all of the vivid colors. These colors do not disappear in umber, but are physically present and almost equivalent. This makes umbers very important to architecture, because they can be combined harmoniously with every color. This, along with the following shade, is the most noble of Le Corbusier's purist colors. Terre d'ombre naturelle moyenne or the mid-range, lightened version of natural umber is a balanced, elegant, and stone-like grayish brown that is able to reconcile imbalanced situations in a room.

12 Le Corbusier, 1931; Rüegg, 1997 (reprint, 2006).
13 Beate Epperlein, *Monochrome Malerei* (Nuremberg, 1997), p. 78.

CMYK approximation:
0.10.20.30

RGB approximation:
186.177.156

Spatial qualities:
dynamic and stable in all
light conditions,
particularly beautiful in
low light conditions

Historical pigmentation:
natural umber from Cyprus

Industrial pigmentation:
iron oxide pigments
and chrome oxide green

Facade suitability:
weather-resistant

32.142

Light native umber / Terre d'ombre naturelle claire

A shade of Le Corbusier's color palette from 1931[14]

"Each colour possesses degrees where its richness, its opulence on the one hand, its signification on the other, attain an obvious qualification" wrote Le Corbusier. The dark-to-light scale of umbers, ranging from dark gray 32.140, 32.141, 32.142, 32.143, to 32.014 (the lightest color is included among the whites), is less opulent than a means of effecting a useful gradation of shadows. This halftone derivative of umber stabilizes itself in a room. Le Corbusier called it "sand." It could as easily be called "velvet" or "discretion." It is a color that combines all other colors within it. Its rich quality can be experienced in a many-facetted dialog with the environment.

14 Le Corbusier, 1931; Rüegg, 1997 (reprint, 2006).

CMYK approximation:
5.10.20.10

RGB approximation:
220.210.189

Spatial qualities:
dynamic and stable in all
light conditions,
particularly beautiful in
low light conditions

Historical pigmentation:
natural umber from Cyprus

Industrial pigmentation:
iron oxide pigments
and chrome oxide green

Facade suitability:
weather-resistant

32.143

Pale native umber / Terre d'ombre naturelle pâle

A lightened version of 32.142 Terre d'ombre naturelle claire

The Japanese aesthete Jun'ichiro, whose book entitled *In Praise of Shadows* shows how to make interior design more beautiful by infusing it with simplicity, writes about sand walls, and means walls that are painted in a reserved and discrete manner. "We never tire of the sight, for to us this pale glow and these dim shadows far surpass any ornament [...] these delicate differences in the hues of the wall, the shadows in each room take on a tinge peculiarly of their own. In fact, the beauty of a Japanese interior relies fully on the nuances of shadow."[15] This light shade of umber is a shadow color that is confident and self-assured. It is as stylish and discrete as its darker relative.

15 Tanizaki Jun'ichiro, *In Praise of Shadows*
    (Tokyo, 1933 and New York, 2001), p. 9–10.

The Bronzes and Metallics How is it possible to know with any
certainty what effect a color will have on a surface?

There are three different ways to answer this question, each of which examines
different aspects. The more agreement there is among conclusions arrived at by
pursuing these methods, the more certain it is that the newly painted surface will
correspond to one's expectations.

The most objective approach of the three also happens to be the most
neglected in the age of information, and has become, by now, the least known: it
concerns the physical and material level. This consideration yields insight into the interaction between colored pigments and light. From this point of view, any color
is beautiful that can unfold its unique qualities under the given light without altering
the perception of spatial proportions in a negative sense.

The next approach, based on the psychology of color perception, dominates
in today's world. Its insights are objective within the framework of the study, but
if these insights are taken out of context and transformed into generalizations, this
realm becomes a pseudo-science. Used seriously, this point of view lets any color be
beautiful that creates a pleasing atmosphere in the context of its actual use. Generally
accepted interpretations of psychological color meaning will be called "primary
associations" in the following text. They differ from the purely subjective "secondary
associations," which are individual. Examples of primary associations are those
that associate blue with the sky and sea, or green with landscape.

The third approach examines the meanings that are shaped by cultural values
and these individual preferences. Since deductions made using this approach are
the least objective of the three, and also overshadow the other levels, they should be
given unconditional power of veto. If someone is convinced that a certain color is
unlucky, it makes no sense to pursue it—regardless of how well the color would work
with the light and the form in a broader context of meaning.

These three approaches to color selection can be understood and put to use
by studying the colors in the subsequent two chapters. In this chapter on colors
made from bronze and aluminum pigments, the physical properties are in full agreement
with the primary associations. There is little risk of surprise involved with using these
colors. This is not true for the colors presented in the next chapter on the yellows.

"A worthless material like burlap is raised to a higher existential level with a bit of gold dust."
Beate Epperlein [1] on Yves Klein's monochromes in gold

The physical, material, and associative properties of yellow are not in agreement, which is why working with yellow is more difficult. The sixth chapter on the ochers offers plausible, often disregarded solutions to problems that commonly arise with yellow.

Pigments made from bronze and aluminum come in the form of small leaves that align themselves like small mirrors under the painter's brush and, thus, reflect light in a room. Even candlelight suffices to generate a mirror-like effect and in bright daylight, the effect can be staggering. Such knowledge of the material aspects of a color often has consequences for the design, because the surface effect of such colors is dependent on the alignment of the reflecting pigments.

Primary associations link metallic colors to wealth, power, triumph, nobility, crowns, coins, and medals—all of which are associations that do not contradict the luster and spatial presence of the metallic pigments. A dynamic, brilliant effect of the colored surface is guaranteed, irrespective of conditions of light.

---

1 Beate Epperlein, *Monochrome Malerei. Zur Unterschiedlichkeit der vermeintlich Ähnlichen* (Nuremberg, 1997), p. 86.

Pantone approximation:
8002 C

RGB approximation:
138.131.124

Spatial qualities:
passive and stable under
all light conditions

Historical pigmentation:
--

Industrial pigmentation:
stabilized brass

Facade suitability:
not weather-resistant

04.001

Champagne silver / Bronze argenté champagne

Pia Schmid, architect, 2004

Champagne silver is less a color than a haptic experience. It is applied to a
surface with a brush and looks matt and luxurious, as if it was made of silk thread.
The limitations of broadly interpreting any grayish, non-vivid color as belonging
to the element "metal" become evident with surfaces such as this. The oversimplified
notion that any color that appears to be grayish will have a similar effect on space,
regardless of its origins and whether it is made using metallic, gray or umber pigments,
is quite absurd. If this kind of generalization were conveyed to music, it would mean
that an A, which pulses at 440 Mhz, would always sound the same, whether it is
generated by a cello, a piano, or an electric guitar. The color of Champagne silver can
be imitated with umber, but a surface made with the leafing metal pigment does not
take on the earthy quality of umber, but rather that of fabric interwoven with metal
thread, such as brocade. In contrast to the other metallics described here, Champagne
silver is more discrete due to its matt quality and its umber-like hue. It is the epitome
of understatement.

Pantone approximation:
877 C

RGB approximation:
170.170.170

Spatial qualities:
passive and stable under
all light conditions

Historical pigmentation:
stabilized aluminum

Industrial pigmentation:
stabilized aluminum

Facade suitability:
weather-resistant in some
techniques

04.002

Aluminum glaze / Laque métallisée aluminium

A color of the Baumann Prase color card from 1912[2]

Although aluminum is the third most commonly found element of the earth's crust, it is expensive, since a complex process is required to convert bauxite into its useful form. To produce aluminum pigments, aluminum oxide is dissolved and molten, then reduced to the pure metal. From this, the leafing metal pigments are extracted. This creates a brilliant, metallic-colored powder that allows a futuristic-looking effect on surfaces painted with two coats to arise. Light falling on the surface of the pigment is reflected, making the surface appear bright and metallic. When light hits the edges of the leafing pigments, the color appears much darker. The most beautiful effects are created if this paint is brush-applied to the surface, so that all the pigment particles align. Aluminum is the only metallic shade shown here that is suitable for facades.

2 Otto Prase, *Baumanns Neue Farbtonkarte System Prase*
(Aue/Saxony, 1912).

Pantone approximation:
8641 C

RGB approximation:
147.133.57

Spatial qualities:
dynamic, also convincing
in low light conditions

Historical pigmentation:
stabilized brass

Industrial pigmentation:
stabilized brass

Facade suitability:
not weather-resistant

05.001

Gold bronze / Bronze d'or

A color of the Baumann Prase color card from 1912 [3]

Yves Klein, a master of monochrome art, dedicated his last work to Saint Rita, patron saint of hopeless causes. A divided box made of Plexiglas contained gold, ultramarine blue, and bright rose pigments. In this trilogy, gold symbolized the materialization of light. With Gold bronze, the architect has a color that can convey light into subdued areas, because the pigment particles reflect the available light into the interior of the space. "A faint golden glow cast into the enveloping darkness like the glow upon the horizon at dusk [...] How in such a dark place gold draws so much light to itself is a mystery to me. But I can see why in ancient times statues of the Buddha were gilt with gold and why gold leaf covered the walls of the homes of nobility."[4] This quote exemplifies the value of gold as a metal and bronze as a pigment. The purity, shine, and warmth inherent in golden colors have made them a symbol for the sun, light, and wisdom in almost every culture. Gold is superior to bronze since it does not corrode, but its effect in a room can be wonderfully illustrated using bronze. Both optimize light effects and give luminosity to surfaces that are in dark spaces.

3 Ibid.
4 Tanizaki Jun'ichiro, *In Praise of Shadows*
  (Tokyo, 1933 and New York, 2001), p. 22.

Pantone approximation:
8962 C

RGB approximation:
160.120.43

Spatial qualities:
dynamic, also convincing
in low light conditions

Historical pigmentation:
stabilized brass

Industrial pigmentation:
coated mica-based pigment

Facade suitability:
not weather-resistant

08.002

Copper bronze / Bronze cuprique

A color of the Baumann Prase color card from 1912 [5]

Tin was added to copper for the first time in 300 BC, marking the beginning of the bronze era. Bronze was subsequently used to make new tools, bells, and jewelry. As early as 1200, the monk Theophilus described several bronze foundries. The different nuances of bronze that range from pale gold to red-gold are created by a process of alloying. The higher the copper content in the alloy, the redder the bronze. In terms of symbolism, the bronzes represent wealth and femininity. More copper shifts this symbolism towards the feminine. Such symbolism, which is more based on material rather than metaphysical qualities, can easily be conveyed to architectural space. With skilled craftsmanship, the sensual red cast of copper bronze on a surface is quite unique and glamorous.

5 Epperlein, 1997.

The Yellows

According to Goethe's *Theory of Colours*, yellow, orange, and red tend to the "plus" side because they are the "lively and aspiring" colors.[2] Blue, red-blue (violet), and blue-red (purple) tend to the "minus" side. This discrimination is essential to color design. A greenish tint can give yellow an unpleasant effect, especially if the light conditions are unfavorable. "By a slight and imperceptible change, the impression of fire and gold is transformed into one not undeserving the epithet foul; and the colour of honour and joy reversed to that of ignominy and aversion."[3]

"If, however, this colour in its pure and bright state is agreeable and gladdening, and in its utmost power is serene and noble, it is, on the other hand, extremely liable to contamination, and produces a very disagreeable effect if it is sullied, or in some degree tends to the minus [green] side."

Johann Wolfgang von Goethe [1]

Eva Heller calls yellow "the most ambiguous color." On the one hand experience tells us it is symbolically positive, meaning "it symbolizes the sun, light, and everything golden. But historically, it is symbolically negative. Yellow was the color of outlaws, it was the symbolic color of egotistic characteristics."[4] What did Goethe actually observe? Why is yellow particularly ambivalent, and what does that mean for architecture and for walls or facades painted yellow?

Taking a look at yellow coloring materials yields important insights. Yellow pigments absorb light in the short-wave regions of violet and blue. They require high-energy light in order to appear as yellow. Conventional light sources are weak in violet and ultraviolet regions. Moreover, yellow is the brightest color of the visible spectrum. If its luminosity is reduced by shadow (such as with yellow felt, woodchip wallpapers, or textured plaster-finished surfaces), the yellow pigments and the human eye both react strongly to the dimming effect. There is a massive difference between a lit yellow surface and one that is shaded. Goethe was describing this phenomenon in his writings.

The most powerful association to yellow, which is shared by cultures all over the world, is the sun. If this association is conveyed to architectural spaces and the described material properties of yellow pigment are not taken into consideration, one may be tempted to design the room to be "sunny" and warm by painting it yellow. The physical interaction of yellow pigments with light will make this plan fail, the result will not be convincing, and the negative associations with yellow as an ostracized color will be most evident if the yellow surface does not find the conditions it needs in order to radiate its beauty.

This discrepancy can be overcome by choosing a yellow color shade from a palette that avoids pure yellows and favors either reddish yellows, being warm and obliging, regardless of light conditions, grayed yellows, being inherently stable in the shade, or even gold.

Yellow advances in space and imposes itself while gray is more taciturn. Yellow colors need the most light in order to be luminous; blue and gray demand the least. The following generalizations may thus be drawn for defining space with yellow:

– Well lit yellow walls in large rooms will appear bright and sunny.

– Yellow surfaces advance in space, yellow rooms will appear to be smaller.

– Surfaces that have a rough plaster finish and those in shadow will be pleasing, if a reddish or grayish yellow is applied.

– Smooth surfaces in shaded areas will have a very noble effect if gold leaf or bronze and metallic colors are used.

1 Johann Wolfgang von Goethe, *Theory of Colours* (London, 1840), section 770, p. 308
2 Goethe (1840), section 264, p. 306.
3 Goethe (1840), section 771, p. 308.
4 Eva Heller, *Wie Farben wirken. Farbpsychologie, Farbsymbolik, kreative Farbgestaltung*, (Reinbek near Hamburg, [2]2005), p. 129.

CMYK approximation:
0.55.100.0

RGB approximation:
215.145.36

Spatial qualities:
dynamic even in low light
conditions

Historical pigmentation:
chrome red and chrome
yellow

Industrial pigmentation:
mixture of organic
and inorganic pigments with
complementary elements

Facade suitability:
not weather-resistant

43.22

Persian orange / Orange perse

Günther Förg, artist, 2002

Günther Förg discovered Persian orange while looking for a color somewhere
between 43.17 Orange and 43.20 Jaune vif by Le Corbusier. Persian orange is an old
color: the Burinmo hunters in Papua New Guinea first used the term *wor* to describe
this yellowish orange with elements of brown and green.[5] In most cases, the colors
and color drawings of native peoples reflected colors that were based on those found
in the natural environment. Persian orange is similar to the color of the blossoms
of the marigold family. It is a harmonious, green-gold-yellow shade that remains stable
even in low light conditions. Today's demand for efficiency has produced increasingly
luminous, monochrome colors that sometimes react unpleasantly to changes in
light sources. Natural, complex combinations of colors, such as Persian orange, are
luminous in all light conditions, because the presence of all other colors within
them allows them to react to changes in daylight or artificial light in a more different-
iated manner.

5 Simon Ings, *A Natural History of Seeing. The Art and Science of Vision*
   (New York, 2007), p. 213.

CMYK approximation:
10.0.65.0

RGB approximation:
232.237.128

Spatial qualities:
dynamic, even in low light
conditions

Historical pigmentation:
Litholechtgrüngelb G

Industrial pigmentation:
bismuth yellow, chrome
green, and ocher

Facade suitability:
weather-resistant in some
techniques

32.065

Bauhaus yellow / Jaune "Bauhaus"

Hans Kittel, color card in the book entitled *Pigmente*, 1960[6]

Wassily Kandinsky divided colors into "two sweeping categories [...]. 1. According to the color's quality of warmth or cold and, 2. its quality of lightness and darkness."[7] Most of the yellows can be designated as warm and light. The last color in this chapter, 08.004 Jaune ocre, could be characterized as neutral and dark, while a lemon yellow would be cool and light. Bauhaus yellow is cold and dark, which makes it an exception among the yellow tones. Fritz Pfister, who gave his name to the German term for this color, was the first to re-create the oldest BASF color, *Litholechtgrüngelb G*, from modern yellow pigments. The somewhat cool color tone can unfold elegantly in light, but is rather dull in shaded areas. It works excellently with metallic blues, with grays, or with the umbers. The fascination of the color lies in its acerbity. It recalls the yellow-green lichen on weathered rocks more than the yellow of an egg yolk or the sun.

---

6 Hans Kittel, *Pigmente. Herstellung, Eigenschaften, Anwendung* (Stuttgart, 1960).
7 Wassily Kandinsky, *Über das Geistige in der Kunst* (Bern, 1952) (original edition 1910).

CMYK approximation:
0.0.40.0

RGB approximation:
254.250.181

Spatial qualities:
dynamic

Historical pigmentation:
organic yellow pigment
with red ocher, and raw
umber

Industrial pigmentation:
bismuth yellow, with red and
green pigments

Facade suitability:
weather-resistant in some
techniques

32.066

Primrose yellow / Jaune primevère

Lightening of the color 43.20 Jaune vif, 2002

"If I say yellow and blue, I do not mean a flat yellow and a flat blue, like the animals depicted in school books or encyclopedias. Naturally, as a painter I mean twenty nuances of yellow and twenty of blue."[8] Giacometti was right, because when examined closely it is evident that the yellow of the primrose, like all the colors of nature, contains many different nuances. The palette within Primrose yellow ranges from the gentle green end of the yellow spectrum to the orange reds. This transition from green to red makes yellows particularly sensitive to light because yellow pigments are the least robust. Goethe wrote, "Colours are the deeds and sufferings of light,"[9] and meant that color and light must be interpreted together. The blossoms need the sun in spring to gain strength, and from this it follows that Primrose yellow needs direct light so as not to appear fragile.

8 Translated from Augusto Giacometti, *Blätter der Erinnerung* (Chur, 1997), p. 198
9 Goethe (1840), preface, p. 315.

CMYK approximation:
0.15.75.0

RGB approximation:
245.220.98

Spatial qualities:
dynamic, less luminous in
the shade

Historical pigmentation:
Naples yellow 725 light

Industrial pigmentation:
bismuth yellow or Hansa
yellow with complementary
elements

Facade suitability:
not weather-resistant

32.068

Naples yellow (color shade) / Jaune de Naples

Hans Kittel, color card in the book entitled *Pigmente*, 1960 [10]

Early on, Cennini described a mineral-based yellow, called Giallorino di fornace (*Ofengelb*, or oven yellow), that was later used as a color for fine art paints in Naples during the Renaissance. The Italian name refers to the manufacturing process, which entails roasting antimony ore. The lead-based antimony pigment had a low tinting-strength and it was expensive, but it was opaque and could be used in almost every binder. It is a cultural companion of mankind, although the name Naples yellow first appeared after 1700. It was used in high-quality interior and exterior oil paints, used, for example, on the underside of the roof of Bauhaus instructors Muche and Schlemmer's house in Dessau. Here the decorative, lead-based pigment conserved the wood. Today, the friendly, balanced quality of Naples yellow is made with a lead-free pigment mixture.

[10] Kittel, 1960.

CMYK approximation:
0.25.95.0

RGB approximation:
233.201.47

Spatial qualities:
dynamic, needs good light
to be radiant, dull in shaded
areas

Historical pigmentation:
chrome yellow

Industrial pigmentation:
organic and inorganic
mixture of pigments with
complementary elements

Facade suitability:
not weather-resistant

43.20

Bright yellow / Jaune vif

A shade of Le Corbusier's color palette from 1959 [11]

In his seminal color palette for architecture, the so-called architectural *grande
gamme*, Le Corbusier did not include yellow among those colors that remain stable in
space to support architecture's three-dimensional effects. "A square meter of yellow
dominates four times its surface area," wrote Le Corbusier's friend Fernand Léger. [12]
A strong yellow, such as Jaune vif, is too forceful; its dynamic quality is too dependant
on light. Jaune vif is a sunny yellow shade that is as cheerful when well lit as it is
disappointing in the shade. This is due to the fact that potentially strong yellow pigments need high-frequency light in order to unfold. This is missing in shaded areas,
which makes the room look twice as bleak. Paints made with metallic, light-reflecting
bronze pigments and the less demanding ochers are more likely to infuse a dark
space with brightness and warmth.

11 Le Corbusier, *Claviers de Couleurs Salubra 2* (Basel 1959).
    See also Arthur Rüegg (ed.), *Polychromie architecturale. Le Corbusiers Farbenklaviaturen von 1931 und 1959/
    Le Corbusier's Color Keyboards from 1931 and 1959/Les claviers de couleurs de Le Corbusier de 1931 et de 1959*
    (Basel, Boston, Berlin, 1997) (reprint, 2006).
12 *Léger and Purist Paris*, exhibition catalog, ed. The Tate Gallery (London 1970), p. 96.

CMYK approximation:
0.15.80.10

RGB approximation:
221.202.80

Spatial qualities:
dynamic, effective in the
shade

Historical pigmentation:
Naples yellow with raw umber

Industrial pigmentation:
bismuth yellow, ocher, and
umber

Facade suitability:
weather-resistant in some
techniques

08.004

Yellow ocher / Jaune ocre

Le Corbusier, Maison Blanche, La Chaux-de-Fonds, 1912

The yellower and purer its hue, the more light will a yellow need to be cheerful.
A grayish-yellow tone is warmer and more calming than a pure yellow, which perpetually
requests that you "turn on the light." The presence of yellow makes a color tend
towards the light, the presence of gray lends it stability in shade. Light and yellow go
hand in hand; both are necessary at once. The demand for yellow in a poorly lit
space may be fulfilled with gold or, alternatively, with a grayish-yellow such as Jaune
ocre. The shadowy Yellow ocher can be traced to Le Corbusier's bedroom in the
Maison Blanche. The raw umber it contains, which is beautiful under any conditions,
balances the light-demanding, mineral-based yellow pigment. The resultant color
is light-stable, harmonious, and pleasant.

The Ochers

Ocher is the term used for a palette of colors made with iron pigments that range from light sand to autumnal, dark, straw-like shades. Jarman's statement about brown is even more appropriate to ocher, because ocher is actually a darkened yellow. In color design books, it is even rarer as an independent color than brown is. An exception is the book *Paint and Paper. A Masterclass in Colour and Light* by David Oliver.[2] In his publication, Oliver highlights simple ocher nuances as colors that are gentler, warmer, and more primeval than lemon yellow.

"It confuses theorists. And is conspicuous by its absence in colour books. What is brown's kinship with yellow? Is brown mixed, as some have said, in the eyes? No monochromatic wavelength exists for brown. Brown is a sort of darkened yellow."
Derek Jarman[1]

Ocher pigments were originally derived from natural sources. Yellow ochers, the most common pigments in the earth's crust, form clusters that range in color from pale yellow and reddish-yellow to brownish-red. Although common, ocher deposits tend to be small, the clusters and mineral deposits rarely extensive. Discovering a "deeply colored ocher" was long considered "a matter of great value,"[3] and the most beautiful ochers were often named after their source, such as Thuringia, Kitzingen, Rome, or Siena. The marginal income to be obtained from the small deposits caused problems in pigment and paint production, since the color quality and the yields varied from mine to mine. From about 1950 onward, burgeoning industries began producing synthetic iron oxide pigments, which were more consistent in yield and quality. The ocher-colored iron oxide pigments often named mars yellow could, as an added benefit, be used with any binder, and they were so opaque that they successively replaced the natural ochers between 1953 and 1993. The synthetic oxidation products made from iron cuttings are heavy, dark in color, and dull compared to the luminous, natural ochers, since the natural pigments contain less iron and more quartz crystals and lime.

Regardless of the pigment's origins, all iron pigments are effective under low light conditions, which is why colors made from ocher are excellent for use in shadowed areas. Ochers are able to do what is often expected from pure shades of yellow. Common associations of ochers to desert sand, humus, straw, and sun-bleached bones reflect this capability. Recommendations to use yellow to bring light to dark spaces may be fulfilled using unassuming ochers, or light-reflective leafing bronzes. A natural sand shade will evoke the beach or sun better than a sunshine yellow color, which, under conditions of low light, will look faded and greenish. The often-disappointed assumption that yellow colors bring warmth and sun to a space results from the all-too broadly generalized color term yellow, which ranges from lime yellow to ocher to golden yellow. In fact, the primary color yellow in Munsell's 1908 color wheel was made using the inimitable pigment raw Sienna,[4] as was his fabulous light olive green, which was made with Guignet's green and Sienna.

A closer inspection of the materials available reveals that the yellow used for centuries in architecture was not a bright yellow, but ocher. Thus, many do not know that the term yellow in the literature from before 1940 often meant "ocher," and that statements about the effect of ocher were often unwittingly conveyed to yellow. Yellow paints, bright and luminous shades of color made with demanding pigments, will shine brightly only under conditions of good lighting. Ochers, sandy shades made with unostentatious iron oxides, are warm and beautiful even in the shade.

1   Derek Jarman, *Chroma. A Book of Colour* (London, 1994), p. 81.
2   David Oliver, *Paint and Paper. A Masterclass in Colour and Light* (London, 2007).
3   Josef Bersch, *Die Fabrikation der Erdfarben* (Vienna, Leipzig, ³1918), p. 29.
4   Albert H. Munsell, *Color Notation* (Boston, 1905).

CMYK approximation:
5.15.40.20

RGB approximation:
197.184.140

Spatial qualities:
passive and stable under
all light conditions

Historical pigmentation:
Sienna clair

Industrial pigmentation:
iron oxide yellow with umber

Facade suitability:
weather-resistant

09.001

Sahara sand deep / Sahara foncé

Kitzinger platinum color card, circa 1910

The Kitzinger pigment factory, purveyor to the Kingdom of Bavaria, produced a small color card some time before World War I, consisting of natural earth shades. Only two brighter green shades, colors similar to 32.040 Vert foncé and 32.050 Vert vif 2, were added to the amiable satin ocher, red ocher, and maroon shades and their lighter pastels. In addition to the classic yellow ochers, there were two rather greenish dark ochers in the series. Like the umbers, they contain admixtures of yellow, white, red, black, and green particles, thus they have many of the same advantages. The pigment of French origin this color is derived from is called either Sienna clair or Sahara sand, and it is a calcareous, finely crystalline natural earth with a unique shade of color. In the pure form displayed here, it evokes memories of the dry, wind-swept sands of the Sahara desert.

CMYK approximation:
5.15.40.10

RGB approximation:
217.201.153

Spatial qualities:
passive and stable under
all light conditions

Historical pigmentation:
Sienna clair

Industrial pigmentation:
iron oxide yellow, titanium
white, and umber

Facade suitability:
weather-resistant

09.002

Sahara sand medium / Sahara moyen

Kitzinger platinum color card, circa 1910

Combining the clay-like, rather grayed, yellow Sienna earth named Sahara with white chalk generates light pastels that lend a surface a special ambiance. They are naturally grayer and more similar to clay plasters than other ocher nuances, giving them a more withdrawn and discriminating quality. They build a bridge from the light ochers to the shady green umbers. As is the case with all pastels, the choice of the white pigment is important. This lightened shade, no. 208 on the Kitzinger color card of oil paints, was produced from natural Sahara with lead white. The optical depth and warmth of lead white can be attained in aqueous systems by using Champagne chalk as the white pigment. Using conventional titanium white to lighten Sahara overwhelms and dulls the color, unless umber is added to soften the texture and enhance the color depth of the pastel shade in amounts proportional to the amount of the universal color-killer titanium white added.

CMYK approximation:
0.5.30.10

RGB approximation:
231.222.178

Spatial qualities:
passive and stable under
all light conditions

Historical pigmentation:
Sienna clair

Industrial pigmentation:
iron oxide yellow, titanium
white, and umber

Facade suitability:
weather-resistant

09.003

Light Sahara sand / Sahara clair

Villa La Roche, gallery, color scheme, 1936

An exceptionally attractive, velvety gradation of the Sahara pigment was found under six newer layers of paint in the gallery of the Villa La Roche in Paris, built between 1923 and 1925 by Le Corbusier and Pierre Jeanneret. The lightest and most calming derivative of the clay-like, natural pigment was initially used together with a particularly deep, burnt umber in a second color scheme completed in 1936. The colors used in the picture gallery were Sahara clair, 26.120 Brun rouge LR, 32.012 Gris clair 2, and 26.030 Bleu charron. Sahara clair covered the largest surface and also established the quietude of the space, in which owner Raoul La Roche hung his collection of paintings by Braque, Picasso, Léger, and other exponents of the lively Parisian art scene in the 1920s.

CMYK approximation:
0.15.30.0

RGB approximation:
245.225.184

Spatial qualities:
passive and stable under
all light conditions

Historical pigmentation:
Sienna clair

Industrial pigmentation:
iron oxide yellow with umber

Facade suitability:
weather-resistant

32.060

Light ocher / Ocre clair

A shade of Le Corbusier's color palette from 1931[5]

The crystalline iron oxide-based natural Sienna pigment from which this shade of Light ocher is made allows extraordinarily luminous, long-lasting distemper and lime paints to be produced. Natural types of ocher are divided into three categories: lean (i.e. gypsum-rich), calcareous ochers such as Ocra limone, which are good for glue-bound distemper paints; unctuous, clay-rich ochers, such as those from Roussillon, which are good for oil paints (they will stick to your tongue and feel soft to the touch), and quartz-rich ochers, such as raw Sienna, which are good for finishing plasters and lime washes. The geological genesis of raw Sienna gives it a crystal structure with planes and prisms that refract and reflect the light, much like a rough diamond does. The reserved elegance of this color and the durability of the paint it made allowed this sandy, warm nuance to become a perennial favorite in living rooms and on facades. Raw Sienna was architecture's true "yellow" until approximately 1940.

5 Le Corbusier, *Claviers de Couleurs Salubra* (Basel, 1931).
  See also Arthur Rüegg (ed.), *Polychromie architecturale. Le Corbusiers Farbenklaviaturen von 1931 und 1959/ Le Corbusier's Color Keyboards from 1931 and 1959/ Les claviers de couleurs de Le Corbusier de 1931 et de 1959* (Basel, Boston, Berlin, 1997) (reprint, 2006).

CMYK approximation:
0.10.35.0

RGB approximation:
248.233.181

Spatial qualities:
passive and stable under
all light conditions

Historical pigmentation:
ocra limone

Industrial pigmentation:
burnt iron oxide yellow

Facade suitability:
weather-resistant

32.061

Yellow limonite ocher / Ocre jaune limone

Gottfried Semper, Waschschiff Treichel, 1861[6]

A yellow stone from Italy, low in iron but high in anhydrite, yields the ocra limone
pigment used in this bright, clear, and transparent ocher variety. Ocra limone allows
surfaces to appear vivid, sandy and gently illuminated. The color Ocre jaune limone is
the least earthy of all the shades in this ocher series. When ordering the natural
ocher color palette from light to dark and from light ocher over pale ocher, dark ocher,
stone ocher, golden ocher, to brown ocher, then Ocre jaune limone will be located
at the light ocher end of the spectrum. Gottfried Semper's Treichel Waschschiff (a boat
on the river in which garments were washed before the advent of washing machines)
was reconstructed in 2003 by Burkhalter und Sumi. The exterior polychromy relies on
the timeless combination of Ocre jaune limone and Pompeian red to create a strong
dynamic contrast.

6 Mark Angélil, Sarah Graham, Reto Pfenninger, and Manuel Scholl,
 Waschanstalt Zürich-Wollishofen (Sulgen / Zurich, 2001).

CMYK approximation:
0.20.40.0

RGB approximation:
241.214.162

Spatial qualities:
passive and stable under
all light conditions

Historical pigmentation:
Ocre Pussigny JSLEF

Industrial pigmentation:
iron oxide yellow with umber

Facade suitability:
weather-resistant

32.062

Pussigny Ocher / Ocre Pussigny

A traditional color, component of every palette until circa 1950

For centuries, producers of opulent paints treasured the pigments found in
the ocher mines of Burgundy, France. Locations in Roussillon in the south of France
yield ocher nuances that are particularly rich in clay and deep in color, with colors
ranging from dark ocher to golden ocher. The pigment used in the shade displayed
here originates from the cliffs near Pussigny, a small town on the Loire. For centuries,
the Société des Ocres[7] has marketed a large variety of French ochers, pigments
that are experiencing a well-deserved renaissance today. The most important quality
features are classified by a system of letters. The French ocher used for this shade
is labeled JSLEF: J=jaune (yellow), S=supérieur (best sort), L=lavé (washed), E=extra,
F=foncé (dark). The austere beauty of the color is representative of the landscape
from which it originates. Under the microscope, this beauty is echoed in the remarkable
mineral composition containing iron oxide, manganese oxide, silica, clay, limestone,
and magnesium.

7 Société des Ocres de France, www.ocres-de-france.com.

CMYK approximation:
0.35.50.10

RGB approximation:
212.170.120

Spatial qualities:
static and stable under
all light conditions

Historical pigmentation:
ocre masson JSE

Industrial pigmentation:
iron oxide yellow with
iron oxide red

Facade suitability:
weather-resistant

32.064

Reddish ocher / Ocre rose

A traditional color, a component of every palette until circa 1950

Ocher is a brown hematite mixed intimately with clay, quartz, and sand. Iron oxides give the mixture of minerals its characteristic, reddish-yellow color. Reddish ocher pigment was originally obtained from iron sludge. Such ochers were typically found in volcanic regions like Wehr, in the Eifel mountain range in western Germany and eastern Belgium. The area boasts carbonated springs that carried iron particles to the surface and created sedimentary iron deposits in the volcanic moors. The color of Reddish ocher originated in the volcanic embers when water evaporated from yellow ocher to create a more reddish tone. It is an interesting fact that the ocher mining trade in Wehr, which ceased in 1957, has been almost completely forgotten today, the more vivid natural pigments having been replaced on a wide scale by synthetic iron oxides. Reddish ocher is particularly effective when combined with muted grays and greens.

CMYK approximation:
0.30.60.0

RGB approximation:
234.194.119

Spatial qualities:
passive and stable under
all light conditions

Historical pigmentation:
mars yellow

Industrial pigmentation:
iron oxide yellow

Facade suitability:
weather-resistant

43.11

Gold ocher / Ocre jaune clair

A shade of Le Corbusier's color palette from 1959[8]

Ivory white, two ochers, and two medium grays supplement the fifteen saturated nuances of Le Corbusier's second color collection designed for the Salubra wall paper company in 1959. The colors of the construction materials inherent to the impressive concrete buildings of the 1950s required a more saturated palette. Le Corbusier's keyboard, the design of which allowed all colors to be paired equally, was based on a reduction in number and scaling-up in the degree of contrast based on the earlier palette of colors. Ocre jaune clair was one color that was upgraded to a higher level of saturation. The color is derived from a synthetic iron oxide pigment produced from iron cuttings, which is why it is more opaque, deeper, and spatially more present than Le Corbusier's lighter ochers made from raw Sienna. The presence of Ocre jaune clair makes it a good partner for the very strong red tones of the 1950s color chart, such as 43.12 Rouge rubis und 43.1 Rouge vif.

8 Le Corbusier, *Claviers de Couleurs Salubra 2* (Basel, 1959).
See also Arthur Rüegg (ed.), *Polychromie architecturale. Le Corbusiers Farbenklaviaturen von 1931 und 1959 / Le Corbusier's Color Keyboards from 1931 and 1959 / Les claviers de couleurs de Le Corbusier de 1931 et de 1959* (Basel, Boston, Berlin, 1997) (reprint, 2006).

CMYK approximation:
0.15.40.0

RGB approximation:
244.223.167

Spatial qualities:
passive and stable under
all light conditions

Historical pigmentation:
raw Sienna

Industrial pigmentation:
iron oxide yellow

Facade suitability:
weather-resistant

43.15

Light native Sienna / Terre de Sienne claire

A shade of Le Corbusier's color palette from 1959[9]

The so-called natural earth from Siena is often, but not always, mined in Tuscany.
It is purer, more transparent, and more crystalline than other kinds of ocher, since
it contains within its pigment particles more iron oxide and quartz but less limestone
and anhydrite. Since colors made from this natural earth pigment are particularly
luminous and warm, artists working in every technique have valued them for centuries.
The luminous warmth of the Tuscan earth can be easily conveyed to architecture,
and Le Corbusier used clear, raw Sienna in his white, purist spaces repeatedly and
effectively, either as a distemper paint for interior wall surfaces, or as an oil paint
for wood and built-in furniture. Applied to walls as opaque distemper paint, sandy raw
Sienna conveys an atmosphere of coziness, continuity and simplicity.

9 Ibid.

The Oranges

It is often said that orange unites within it the best qualities of yellow and red; it is warm, self-confident, mature, and cheerful. These qualities unfold in space, provided that the surface painted orange is well placed and evenly lit. We have seen that yellow lacks luster and looks gloomy in the shade; gold, with its reflective qualities, appears mystic and more luminous; and ocher, timeless and primal, all under the same conditions of low light. Orange, which is generally a mixture of red and yellow, golden, or ocher pigments, embraces a group of color shades whose strengths need to be regarded individually.

A color with a yellow content will appear to advance in space and it will become sensitive to light. Conversely, a color to which gray is added will no longer advance in space, and it will lose its sensitivity to light. This means that the yellow-gray division among all shades of colors is a highly effective light-shadow division for the color designer. The higher the yellow content in a color, the more dramatic will its loss of brilliance in low light conditions be. The higher the gray content in a color, the greater will its indifference and independence in low light conditions be.

Applying this to orange, it means that muted orange nuances will look more beautiful when placed in the shade than pure ones. Persian orange 43.22 shown in the last chapter of yellows demonstrates that highly saturated but rather muted shades of (non-metallic) gold work well in low light conditions. 43.17 Orange from Le Corbusier's 1950s color palette is a further convincing example of the richness a muted color orange can unfold in the shade. One could therefore speak of a cheerful, rich potential the color orange may have if certain factors are considered. The first is the yellow and gray content; the second, its placement in space and the lighting; the third, its lightness or value, which is a measure of its spatial dynamics; the fourth, its spatial dimensions. This final consideration will be discussed in more detail in connection with the reds. The third attribute of the color, its spatial dynamics, describes the force of a color relative to its maximum energy. How active, intense, or powerful is it compared to the pure shade of the same pigment? Color theorists reduce

"This warming orange is the colour of the robes of Buddhist monks and Christian confessors. It is the colour of maturity."
Derek Jarman[1]

"Color is primarily quality. Secondly, it is also weight, for it has not only color value, but also brilliance. Thirdly it is measure, for besides quality and weight, it has its limits, its area, and its extent, all of which may be measured."
Paul Klee[2]

the intensity by reducing saturation or adding white. For Paul Klee, the spatial dynamics of a particular color was a question of its lightness, which he called its weight. He reduced the weight of a color by making it more transparent, or by adding white. Spatial dynamics, as defined here, refer to the intensity of a surface color relative to its most saturated, undiluted with white, shade. The dynamics are modulated by adding white. We use the term strictly for opaque paints. The spatial dynamics of a color are specified by the amount of white in the hue, which can range from zero, to a little, to much.

An orange that does not contain white, such as 43.22 Persian orange or 43.17 Orange, is active, dynamic, and has a forceful spatial presence. A dark orange such as 43.17 solidifies the surface plane and lets it advance in space. Lighter shades of the same orange, such as 32.080 Orange vif, 32.081 Abricot, or 32.082 Abricot clair, gradually forfeit this highly dynamic spatial effect. The most subtle orange, 32.082 Abricot clair, is so delicate that Le Corbusier categorized it as a passive color, meaning that it is a background color that will not influence our perception of space, instead, it will affect the underlying ambiance. In fact, Abricot clair provides a wall or exterior facade with the warm glow and radiance of light at sunset.

Le Corbusier categorized colors according to their dynamic attributes as defined above: the *major scale* (*grande gamme*) or palette of passive colors consisting of the "ochre yellows, reds [red ochres!], natural earths, white, black, ultramarine blue, and of course certain of their derivatives; this scale is a strong, stable scale giving unity and holding the plane of the picture since these colors keep one another in balance. They are thus essentially constructive colors; it is these colors that all the great periods employed; it is these colors that whoever wishes to paint in volume should use.

The *dynamic scale*, including citron yellow, the oranges (chrome and cadmium), vermilions, Veronese green, light cobalt blues. An essentially animated, agitated scale, giving the sensation of a perpetual change of plane: these colors do not keep to one plane; sometimes they seem in front of the surface plane, sometimes behind it. They are disruptive elements.

Finally there is the *transitional scale*, the madders, emerald green, all the lakes which have properties of tinting, not of construction."[3]
This classification of colors, described during the era of purist paintings, is further differentiated for its use in architecture with the color keyboards from 1931. Le Corbusier now limits the *major scale* of spatially passive nuances to certain light color values. All saturated color shades, even natural earths, are now classified as dynamic. The later color keyboard of the 1950s is composed almost exclusively of such dynamic shades.

1 Derek Jarman, *Chroma. A Book of Colour* (London, 1994), p. 95.
2 Paul Klee, *Paul Klee on Modern Art* (London, 1966), p. 19.
3 Amédée Ozenfant, Charles-Edouard Jeanneret (Le Corbusier), "Le Purisme,"
   in *L'Esprit Nouveau* 4, 1921, quoted from Robert L. Herbert (ed.), *Modern Artists on Art. Ten Unabridged Essays*
   (Englewood Cliffs/NJ, 1964), p. 70.

CMYK approximation:
20.80.90.10

RGB approximation:
157.77.51

Spatial qualities:
dynamic

Historical pigmentation:
red ocher pigment

Industrial pigmentation:
oxide red brightened
with orange

Facade suitability:
weather-resistant in some
techniques

43.23

Spice red / Rouge épice

A color of the Baumann Prase color card from 1912[4]

Recent findings have shown that deep, bright red earth colors such as Spice red symbolized warmth for early humans as long as 125,000 years ago. The Greek primary red color called *Sinopia* is one of these colors. The name *Sinopia* originates from a dry, sandy, brownish-red ocher pigment that was mined in Sinop, possibly the oldest Greek colony near the Black Sea. Authors of studies of Homer's *Iliad* noted that it contains comparatively few color names, and some hypothesized that color perception and color names could be a relatively recent evolutionary development. Later researchers, however, noted that modern color names describe coordinates and locations in a color space and not complex sensory impressions, and concluded that a term like *Sinop* (or other mining locations) could, in fact, be a color name. We now know that the ancient Greeks had a complete compendium of color terms such as *Sinopia*, which did not represent pure spectral colors, but rather complex sensory impressions and statements of origin. A typical color terms is "dry, blazing red earth from Sinop."[5] The effect of Spice red is a powerful one. If a wall should have warmth, be present, and glow in space while being earthy, this color is a wonderful option.

4 Otto Prase, *Baumanns Neue Farbtonkarte System Prase*
(Aue / Saxony, 1912).
5 Simon Ings, *A Natural History of Seeing. The Art and Science of Vision* (New York, 2007), p. 217.

CMYK approximation:
0.75.100.5

RGB approximation:
196.97.38

Spatial qualities:
dynamic

Historical pigmentation:
lead chromate orange

Industrial pigmentation:
DPP[7]-orange, organic yellow,
and umber

Facade suitability:
weather-resistant in some
techniques

43.17

Orange / Orange

A shade of Le Corbusier's color palette from 1959[6]

This shade is roughly equivalent to classic Saturn red made of red lead. The oxidation of red lead, turning it brown, induced paint manufacturers early on to produce
architectural coatings and artists' paints from chrome and cadmium pigments.
These were replaced by organic pigments free of heavy metals in the 1970s. The gray
color of raw concrete and massive dimensions of his *béton brut* architecture inspired
Le Corbusier to include this extreme orange in the second Salubra palette in the 1950s.
When used in small, white rooms, colors like this one would make contrasts be too
stark and spaces appear even smaller. Against the backdrop of a gray architecture of
more generous spaces, 43.17 Orange may even be combined with other saturated,
dynamic colors, such as 43.18 Bleu foncé or even 43.3 Rose (a combination used by
Heidi Weber in the Le Corbusier Museum in Zurich), to create pleasing, harmonious effects.

---

6 Le Corbusier, *Claviers de Couleurs Salubra 2* (Basel, 1959).
  See also Arthur Rüegg (ed.), *Polychromie architecturale. Le Corbusiers Farbenklaviaturen von 1931 und 1959 /
  Le Corbusier's Color Keyboards from 1931 and 1959 / Les claviers de couleurs de Le Corbusier de 1931 et de 1959*
  (Basel, Boston, Berlin, 1997) (reprint, 2006).
7 Abbreviation for Diketopyrrolopyrrole.

CMYK approximation:
0.70.100.0

RGB approximation:
207.113.39

Spatial qualities:
dynamic

Historical pigmentation:
lead chromate orange

Industrial pigmentation:
DPP-orange, organic yellow,
and umber

Facade suitability:
weather-resistant in some
techniques

32.080

Bright orange / Orange vif

A shade of Le Corbusier's color palette from 1931[8]

In the first decades of the twentieth century, many representatives of modernism sincerely hoped that a new style of architecture would influence society and make it a better place to live. Construction forms and building materials changed radically during this period. Hoping to compensate for some of the strangeness of the new architecture, Le Corbusier stayed with the colors of a traditional artists' paint palette, thus anchoring his innovative architecture in the natural color scheme used in classical painting. It was not until the 1960s that a new generation of modernists began to embrace flashy colors in new combinations. Orange vif is part of the classic palette, whose brightest colors even are still balanced and contained. However, the beauty of this youthful color unfolds best when the surface is well lit or in the sun. Used as a dynamic accent against a light gray or white background, Orange vif produces a mood of optimism.

8 Le Corbusier, *Claviers de Couleurs Salubra* (Basel, 1931).
See also Arthur Rüegg (ed.), *Polychromie architecturale. Le Corbusiers Farbenklaviaturen von 1931 und 1959 / Le Corbusier's Color Keyboards from 1931 and 1959 / Les claviers de couleurs de Le Corbusier de 1931 et de 1959* (Basel, Boston, Berlin, 1997) (reprint, 2006).

CMYK approximation:
0.50.70.0

RGB approximation:
220.155.90

Spatial qualities:
dynamic

Historical pigmentation:
lead chromate orange

Industrial pigmentation:
DPP-orange, organic yellow,
and umber

Facade suitability:
weather-resistant in some
techniques

32.081

Apricot / Abricot

A shade of Le Corbusier's color palette from 1931[9]

Artists have traditonally viewed orange colors with skepticism, perhaps because standard mixtures of yellow and red pigments rarely produce attractive colors. More-over, mixed oranges were often compared, and considered inferior, to pure scarlet. Lighter shades of orange are even more difficult to formulate, and rarely beautiful. What is it that makes a color look beautiful? The beauty of an attractive color touches you emotionally, and it fills a space with poetry; it can produce feelings of joy, or an exhilarating silence. Dull, all too sweet, or artificial-looking nuances of the color apricot—made by simply adding white-to-pure-orange pigments—cannot achieve such an effect. If, however, an intricately mixed orange such as 32.080 Orange is lightened with white while adding umber, it is simultaneously given light, shade, and a stable beauty. The result is a beautiful color that glows softly in any light.

9 Le Corbusier, 1931; Rüegg, 1997 (reprint, 2006).

CMYK approximation:
0.15.20.0

RGB approximation:
245.225.202

Spatial qualities:
passive and stable under
all light conditions

Historical pigmentation:
burned gold ocher and chalk

Industrial pigmentation:
iron oxide yellow and red,
titanium white

Facade suitability:
weather-resistant in some
techniques

32.082

Abricot clair / Light apricot

A shade of Le Corbusier's color palette from 1931[10]

With this delicate, subtle orange made from natural ocher and chalk white, we return to Le Corbusier's constructive color scale, to the *grande gamme* of essential background colors. The colors of this scale are "basically constructive," and they support architecture by being passive in space. "The major [constructive scale] alone offers many possibilities" for architects that seek to stabilize and not decorate forms through the application of color.[11] Light pastel color shades such as Abricot clair, since they can be made with natural earth pigments, are luminous, grounded, and above all discreet. The term "sand" was used to describe Abricot clair's mural effect, together with 32.131 Light burnt umber or 20-30.18 Marron clair (made of burnt umber and chalk) and 32.091 Rose clair (made of synthetic vermillion and chalk). All the colors denoted to belong to the mural quality "sand" are not sweet pastel hues at all, they are light natural earth colors.

10 Le Corbusier, 1931; Rüegg, 1997 (reprint, 2006).
11 Carol. S. Eliel, *L'Esprit Nouveau. Purism in Paris, 1918–1925* (New York, 2001), p. 56–57.

CMYK approximation:
5.60.80.20

RGB approximation:
172.110.60

Spatial qualities:
dynamic

Historical pigmentation:
terra sigillata and chalk

Industrial pigmentation:
iron oxide red and yellow,
chrome green

Facade suitability:
weather-resistant

08.010

Autumn gold / Or d'automne

A lightened nuance of 08.011 cognac brown, 2008

Adding white to a translucent pigment, such as the remarkable iron oxide used
in 08.010 Autumn gold, can lead to astonishing results. It comes as no surprise that
older manuals for painters and colorists specified which white pigment to use,
and how much of to add, to a color pigment, in order to retain its inherent beauty. Too
much white, or the wrong white pigment, will generate weak and inexpressive lighter
shades. Many series of tests were needed before defining the color Autumn gold.
It is a remarkable fact that the final group verdict on which pastel shades are the most
expressive and attractive is unambiguous, often even unanimous. In this shade, all
of the aspects of a color are balanced: the clay-like pigment, the symbolic relationship
to terracotta, and the pleasing effect of a painted surface that is attractive and
delightful. It is a popular color for facades.

CMYK approximation:
0.70.90.30

RGB approximation:
155.85.39

Spatial qualities:
dynamic

Historical pigmentation:
terra sigillata and chalk

Industrial pigmentation:
iron oxide red and yellow,
chrome green, and titanium
white

Facade suitability:
weather-resistant

08.011

Cognac brown / Brun cognac

Bayer Leverkusen color card, pigment AC 5046, circa 1960

Terra sigillata, a red iron oxide pigment known as "clay tile red from Lemnos,"
contains more than fifty percent silica and approximately eight percent water. It is
different from all other iron oxide red pigments, in that its color is lighter, grayer
and yellower.[12] Terra sigillata produces luminous nuances that react sensitively
to changes in binder, a fact that can be attributed to the silica crystals that provide
the otherwise dull iron oxides with sensivity and elegance. Light reflected from the
needle-shaped pigment particles allows a singular beauty to shine through. Cognac
brown, originally formulated from a mixture of terra sigillata with some chalk, has
a unique color shade between amber and brick red. Its tendency to advance in space
is minimal, and it unfolds its warmth even in the shade.

12 Josef Bersch, *Die Fabrikation der Erdfarben. Handbuch*
(Vienna, Leipzig, [3]1918), p. 179.

The Reds

It is not surprising that chapters on red are often longer than chapters dedicated to other colors. As can be expected, reds call for a detailed classification. The Freiling / Riedel categories are based on the color wheel and do not classify the natural ocher reds as a separate category. The diversity of red coloring materials, ranging from brownish burnt ochers to bright red pigments used in car paints, are rarely differentiated in studies on color perception, but they are important in considering architectural color design. Thus, Kandinsky's classification is correct from an architectural point of view, in its depiction of a spectrum of reds ranging from orange to reddish orange, brownish red and bluish red. His categories can be substantiated by the specific spatial effects each class exhibits. Based on pigments, tradition, and a cultural perspective, it makes sense to categorize the diversity of reds as follows:

Reds that tend to yellow, such as the vermilions and their pastel shades (this chapter), grayed reds that tend to brown, such as red ocher and their pastel shades (chapter 9), and reds that tend to blue including violet and their pastel shades (chapter 10).

Surfaces painted red gain presence in space, red planes approach the viewer, and red objects appear to be more solid and larger than they are. Observations and suggestions such as: "use red sparingly, and white even more sparingly" (Augusto Giacometti),[3] or "No colour is as territorial; it stakes a claim, is on the alert against the spectrum," and "PAINTERS USE RED LIKE SPICE!" (Derek Jarman)[4] arise from this knowledge.

The third attribute of a color, its expanse, or the number of surfaces it is used on and their dimensions, is especially important when dealing with the powerful reds. Even small amounts of added white will mute the tendency of red to advance in space. It can also be made more discrete by adding green or gray. Muting reds in this manner creates matt and expressive reddish-brown shades that will be

"Red is very rich and varied in its material form. There are many that come to mind: Saturn red, vermilion, English red, madder lake, from the lightest to the darkest shades. Red thus has the ability to retain its fundamental tone, yet to appear characteristically warm or cold. [...] What a wealth of inner possibilities!"
Wassily Kandinsky[1]

"According to Heinrich Freiling, a pioneer of color psychology in Germany, the following associations are attributed to red:
Vermilion (a light red inclining toward orange): fire, Eros, danger, and closeness
Carmine (a darker red containing blue): blood, strength, power, love
Purple: royalty, justice, fairness, distance.
Red will advance and dominate in a space; it is strongly agitating, enlivening, and vital, 'it holds the fullness of life'."
Ingrid Riedel[2]

described in the next chapter. With respect to lightening reds to make pinks, it is clear that no other color is as dynamic as red in its saturated values; conversely, no other color loses as much preponderance and presence by tinting with white.

Goethe noted that the effect of the red color cochenille carmine (a color very similar to 32.100 Rouge carminé) "is as peculiar as its nature. It conveys an impression of gravity and dignity and at the same time of grace and attractiveness. The first in its dark state, the latter in its light attenuated tint; and thus the dignity of age and the amiableness of youth may adorn itself with degrees of the same hue."[5] This shift from dignity to grace is almost a reversal and has interesting consequences for a designer. If a blue, a gray, or an orange is too dark, heavy, or prominent, it is advisable to consider a lightened version of the shade. If a red is too powerful, it is less advisable to replace it with a pink than with red ocher shades, because "the impression of vermilion can be given not just sufficiently, but yet more powerfully, by the use of burnt ocher. In accepting this discipline, we have the certitude of confining color to its hierarchical place…"[6]

1 Translated from Wassily Kandinsky, *Über das Geistige in der Kunst* (Bern, 1952), p. 99 (German original edition, 1910).
2 Translated from Ingrid Riedel, *Farben in Religion, Gesellschaft, Kunst und Psychotherapie* (Stuttgart, 1999), p. 190.
3 Translated from Augusto Giacometti, *Blätter der Erinnerung* (Chur, 1997), p. 197.
4 Derek Jarman, *Chroma. A Book of Colour* (London, 1994), p. 31, 33.
5 Johann Wolfgang von Goethe, *Theory of Colours* (London, 1840), section 796, p. 314.
6 Amédée Ozenfant and Charles-Edouard Jeanneret (Le Corbusier), "Le Purisme," in *L'Esprit Nouveau* 4, 1921, quoted from Robert L. Herbert (ed.), *Modern Artists on Art. Ten unabridged Essays* (Englewood Cliffs/NJ, 1964), p. 63.

CMYK approximation:
0.90.100.45

RGB approximation:
121.36.24

Spatial qualities:
dynamic and stable under all
light conditions

Historical pigmentation:
Pozzuoli earth enhanced

Industrial pigmentation:
red oxide fined with DPP red
and chrome green

Facade suitability:
weather-resistant in some
techniques

32.109

Pompeian red / Rouge pompéien

Known since ancient Roman times. A color from the Baumann Prase color card from 1912 [7]

Red ochers are weathering products of hematite and can be found with varying compositions. Their use can be dated back to before ancient Roman times. Pozzuoli earth is found near Naples. It is a fleshy red, of volcanic origin, and chemically unique in containing anhydrate sulfates. When mixed with lime, the red earth is able to set and harden, which made it a popular building material in ancient Pompeii. Pompeian red is made from Pozzuoli earth and a so-called fining agent. Ox blood, red lead, goat blood, vermilion, and punic wax have all been mentioned as fining agents used to enhance the color—as has the fact that Roman master builders either refused to disclose their knowledge, or conveyed instructions in a form that was unusable. According to Max Doerner, Max Eibner [8] proved by microchemical analysis that the luminous Pompeian red surfaces were based on milk-casein and not wax techniques.

7 Otto Prase, *Baumanns Neue Farbtonkarten System Prase*
(Aue / Saxony, 1912).
8 Max Doerner, *Malmaterial und seine Verwendung im Bilde*
(Stuttgart, 1949), p. 256

CMYK approximation:
0.90.100.30

RGB approximation:
147.43.29

Spatial qualities:
dynamic

Historical pigmentation:
Cerium sulfide red

Industrial pigmentation:
DPP red mixed with green

Facade suitability:
weather-resistant in some
techniques

32.095

Swiss red / Rouge puissant

Arthur Rüegg, architect, 2003

Swiss red is a magnificent darker version of Le Corbusier's 32.090 Rouge foncé.
It is a potent, vermilion red shade, with simultaneous tinges of blue and yellow. The
secret behind this color: it is a deep red, but not a pure one. In contrast to a pure
red, which causes the chemical saturation of the cones in the eye, thus tiring people
and forcing them to seek regeneration, Swiss red is neither pure, nor tiring. Such
deep, physiologically pleasing red shades of color are formulated by adding generous
amounts of complementary green pigments to the red to balance the color. Nature
uses this practice in her astonishingly beautiful world of floral colors. As is the case
with all deep reds, this color advances and fixes the surface in space.

CMYK approximation:
0.100.100.30

RGB approximation:
143.0.29

Spatial qualities:
dynamic

Historical pigmentation:
synthetic vermilion

Industrial pigmentation:
DPP red mixed with green

Facade suitability:
weather-resistant in some
techniques

32.090

Deep red / Rouge foncé

A shade of Le Corbusier's color palette from 1931[9]

Rarely has a color been written about so often as the deep red mercuric sulfide pigment called vermilion. It can be obtained from natural sources, in which case it is called cinnabar, or synthetically, in which case it is called vermilion. The poor light-fastness of this ancient, much admired pigment soon led chemists to seek adequate replacements. The search was successful. The term *Rouge vermillon* used by Le Corbusier in his sketches had become a trade name given to any exquisitely luminous red color that fulfilled the characteristics of the archetypical red: neither yellow, nor blue, and thus typical for the perception "red." Rouge foncé appears to advance, it shortens space, and it should be used with consideration. Like all powerful red shades, Rouge foncé is most effective in full light.

9 Le Corbusier, *Claviers de Couleurs Salubra* (Basel, 1931).
   See also Arthur Rüegg (ed.), *Polychromie architecturale. Le Corbusiers Farbenklaviaturen von 1931 und 1959 / Le Corbusier's Color Keyboards from 1931 and 1959 / Les claviers de couleurs de Le Corbusier de 1931 et de 1959* (Basel, Boston, Berlin, 1997) (reprint, 2006).

CMYK approximation:
0.10.20.0

RGB approximation:
248.234.207

Spatial qualities:
passive and stable under
all light conditions

Historical pigmentation:
synthetic vermilion with chalk

Industrial pigmentation:
iron oxide red, titanium white,
with chrome green

Facade suitability:
weather-resistant

32.091

Light pink / Rose clair

A shade of Le Corbusier's color palette from 1931[10]

Pink is not particularly popular in Europe: it is rejected by seven percent of
the female, and twelve percent of the male, population.[11] In light of this fact, it is
interesting to note that pink nonetheless did have an important position in both the
Salubra color series and in Le Corbusier's color concepts. On closer inspection,
it turns out that the disagreeable, gaudy pinks available today have nothing in common
with the earthy Rose clair of Le Corbusier's selection. They only share the name.
Le Corbusier created a pink that is less gaudy than gentle and warming, a reserved
shade that stabilizes itself in space and harmonizes well with dark colors such
as gray, brown, and grayish-blue shades like 20-30.5 Bleu Natier. Le Corbusier used
Rose clair for the inner courtyard of the Villa Savoye to lend the cool concrete
balustrade the charming warm quality of brick masonry.

10 Ibid.
11 Eva Heller, *Wie Farben wirken.*
    Farbpsychologie, Farbsymbolik, kreative Farbgestaltung (Reinbek near Hamburg, 1989), p. 115.

CMYK approximation:
0.90.100.25

RGB approximation:
155.46.30

Spatial qualities:
dynamic, better in well-lit
spaces

Historical pigmentation:
synthetic vermilion
with umber

Industrial pigmentation:
DPP red with chrome green
and yellow oxide

Facade suitability:
suitable for facades in some
techniques

43.1

Bright red / Rouge vif

A shade of Le Corbusier's color palette from 1959 [12]

Some colors seem to correspond to a fundamental human yearning. They endure from century to century, never failing to move the viewer. "Of all human endeavors, what will be remembered is not what is useful, but what moves and exhilarates," wrote Le Corbusier in 1957.[13] This statement, of course, also applies to color; and his color selection is rooted in this conviction. The pigmentation of vermilion has experienced quite a number of changes since antiquity: native cinnabar was insignificant by 1920, having been replaced by synthetic vermilion, chrome red, cadmium red, or mordant pigments. Regardless of their source, any of the vermilion red replacements are bound to be the fieriest of all reds. Vermilion reds such as Rouge vif lend surfaces a warmth that attracts the eye and shortens architectural space. Schönberg and Kandinsky aptly compared this color to the sound of fanfare music!

---

12 Le Corbusier, *Claviers de Couleurs Salubra 2* (Basel, 1959).
   See also Arthur Rüegg (ed.), *Polychromie architecturale. Le Corbusiers Farbenklaviaturen von 1931 und 1959 / Le Corbusier's Color Keyboards from 1931 and 1959 / Les claviers de couleurs de Le Corbusier de 1931 et de 1959* (Basel, Boston, Berlin, 1997) (reprint, 2006).
13 Translated from Le Corbusier, *Von der Poesie des Bauens*,
   chosen in collaboration with the author by Hugo Loetscher (Zurich, 1957), p. 12.

CMYK approximation:
0.85.80.15

RGB approximation:
175.64.53

Spatial qualities:
dynamic, better in well-lit
spaces

Historical pigmentation:
synthetic vermilion

Industrial pigmentation:
DPP red and orange with
green added

Facade suitability:
not weather-resistant

43.21

Poppy red / Coquelicot

Günther Förg, artist, 2003

"As for colour, the crux is in the quantity," wrote Fernand Léger in 1924.[14] This
statement is worth considering for the only slightly muted red shade called Coquelicot
or Poppy red. Surfaces painted with Poppy red develop such a strong presence in
a room, that they can seem confrontational or even obtrusive. If used sparingly and with
discernment, Poppy red can have a wonderful effect. "What you read in books about
complementary colors is superficial and shallow," wrote Augusto Giacometti.[15] "We are
told that red and green are complementary colors and work well together. We hear
nothing about the quantity and value; that it depends entirely on these." Giacometti
was implying that a large quantity of a gentle green shade is needed to embed and
balance a small quantity of an expansive red, such as Poppy red. Just think of poppy
flowers! Förg demonstrated his outstanding grasp for effective color combinations
by skillfully combining a small amount of Coquelicot with a much larger surface of its
true complementary color, the matt, mossy, blackish-green, 26.040 Vert noir.

14 Fernand Léger, "Polychromatic Architecture," in *Léger and Purist Paris*,
   published by John Golding, Christopher Green (New York, 1970) p. 96.
15 Translated from Augusto Giacometti, *Blätter der Erinnerung* (Chur, 1997), p. 198

CMYK approximation:
30.90.90.0

RGB approximation:
152.59.55

Spatial qualities:
dynamic

Historical pigmentation:
Cerium sulfide red,
a non-toxic Rhodia pigment

Industrial pigmentation:
DPP red and green

Facade suitability:
not weather-resistant

43.24

Coral red / Rouge corail

Rhone-Poulenc, 1996

Coral red is the purest red in this chapter. The purity of a color is easily assessed by looking at its spectrum of reflectance. One can see which wavelengths of visible light are absorbed by a pigment and which are reflected. A pure color displays straight lines. A very pure red generates a spectral reflectance shaped like the step of a staircase: energy-rich, shortwave light is absorbed completely by the pigment (which is why red surfaces are so warm!) and other light waves are completely reflected, somewhat like ⌐. A grayed red, such as Pompeian red, absorbs some wavelengths across the entire spectrum, somewhat like ╱. Coral red is not a color that is easy to combine with others; it is dominant and advances in space, whereas Pompeian red harmonizes readily with other colors (it can converse in any language), it dominates less, and does not react as sensitively to light or color changes in its surroundings; hence, it is considered "subdued."

CMYK approximation:
0.95.100.30

RGB approximation:
144.27.29

Spatial qualities:
dynamic

Historical pigmentation:
red ocher, DPP red and
greenish umber

Industrial pigmentation:
DPP ruby, DPP red,
iron oxide red

Facade suitability:
suitable for facades in
some techniques

43.25

Garnet red / Rouge grenat

Midway between 32.109 Pompeian red and 43.1 Rouge vif, 2004

"Colour is a complement to the architecture. It serves to enlarge or reduce a
space. It's also useful for adding that touch of magic a place needs," wrote the Mexican
architect Luis Barragán (1902–1988).[16] He was well versed in the use of powerful,
luminous terracotta shades such as this one. Several masonry chips from Barragán's
buildings reveal this color when examined under the microscope. Garnet red lends
weight to a wall, and even neighboring white planes will appear to move slightly out of
the shadows due to the reddish reflection. The three-dimensional quality of space
will be enhanced, and the room will seem smaller. A surface painted with a coat
of saturated Garnet red will be more dynamic, powerful, and significant. This is why
artists use "red like spice."[17] The smaller the number of thus painted surfaces,
the more powerful will their effect be.

16 Danièle Pauly, *Barragán. Space and Shadow, Walls and Colour*
    (Basel, Boston, Berlin, 2002), p. 183 (reprint, 2008).
17 Jarman, 1994.

The Red Ochers and Browns "The impression of vermilion
can be given not just sufficiently, but more powerfully, by the use of burnt ochre."
This sentence by Le Corbusier and Amédée Ozenfant ended the introduction to
the last chapter. Using the more subtle color reduces the risk of disturbing the formal
language of the architecture.

Strong reds have a tendency to impose themselves and expand in space.
Yellow is also expansive in space, but it is less heavy and manifests itself less than red,
even if it covers the same expanse and has the same surface area. If this dominance
is to be controlled or diminished, the red shade can be muted and then lightened.
If reds are only lightened and not muted, they create pink, which is a color very different
from red. It seems younger and less dignified, as Goethe aptly observed. Muting a
red, then making it lighter with white generates quite a different sequence of brownish-
red colors.

The practice of muting a color by adding black began with the rationalization
of paint production during industrialization. For centuries, fine art painters avoided
muting colors such as red or green with black, knowing that this would make the color
be flat and dull. Their goal was to retain the beauty and depth of the color while darkening the hue. The addition of a complementary color such as green umber or chrome
green to a luminous red shifts the transmission curve of the red towards its complement.

"When speaking of the darkening
of colors to make them appear shadowed, it is often said that it is not
advisable to do so by adding black;
this is said to 'dirty' the color, and one
should instead use the complement.
This is true to the extent that the
addition of the complementary color
will, in fact, darken the color; the tint
will not, however, look better than
the one made with black, and it will
often look even worse, since
significant shifts in the tone will be
induced as well."
Wilhelm Ostwald [1]

The red's spectral activity is enhanced in the region of
the spectrum that was less active, thus the green pigment
increasingly balances the red. The addition of black,
the alternative preferred by Ostwald, reduces red's
activity across the entire range of wavelengths, thereby
muting red's "redness" sequentially until almost no
reflectance is left. Adding green thus balances spectral
activity, whereas adding black reduces it.
In his criticism of the "shifts in the tone," Ostwald demonstrates that the then new practice of referencing colors
to a hypothetical color sphere introduced new priorities to
color mixing. Adding a dull green to a luminous red produced a luminous reddish brown, and the shift in the tone

was not an error, it was the strategy. The strategy in industrial mixing, however, was to prevent shifts in color. The measurable reduction of spectral activity by adding black was now less of a problem than the color shift caused by adding the complement; this was now considered a distortion of the color, which shifted the location of the reference on the color sphere down towards black and around the color wheel towards yellow. This additional shift, which allows the darkened reds to be so luminous, implicates motion in three directions: towards the less-saturated center, towards black, and towards yellow. Such a representation, and the mathematical manipulations involved, cannot be solved with a simple color sphere. A spiral would be needed to describe the path that red follows upon adding green to its logical end point, which is a specific gray, and not black. Every color on the color wheel would have its own spiral and its own dark gray endpoint. The structure that results would be an object of beauty, but the programming involved to reference colors and formulate paints would be much more complex than it is today. Thus, modern color spheres use black as the endpoint of the vertical axis and in their color mixing, as did Ostwald; almost all industrially mixed paints are tinted with black.

By virtue of their heterogeneous, mineral-rich composition, natural red ochers have a built-in complementary content. What scientists would consider a lack of purity explains the vivid hue and the color depth associated with several traditional mining locations. Modern paint factories, if they use complementary mixtures at all, generally use chrome green and iron oxide red to create beautiful red brown nuances.

The best technique for lightening colors will be discussed in the introduction to the next chapter. This much for now: light versions of deep dark browns will not lose their sunburned, earthy quality and will not appear to be gaudy or fleshy, not even when they are used on large surfaces.

1 Translated from Wilhelm Ostwald, *Die Maltechnik jetzt und künftig* (Leipzig, 1930) p. 125.

CMYK approximation:
40.85.90.30

RGB approximation:
105.53.43

Spatial qualities:
dynamic and stable under
all light conditions

Historical pigmentation:
burnt Sienna earth

Industrial pigmentation:
red oxide and complementary
pigments

Facade suitability:
weather-resistant

43.4

Burnt native Sienna / Terre de Sienne brûlée

A shade of Le Corbusier's color palette from 1959[2]

Red earth colors rich in iron oxides were essential pigments throughout cultural history until the 1940s. The widespread availability and luminosity of the red hematites ensured their continual presence in the palettes of paints used for the most beautiful artworks and noblest constructions throughout all major eras of art and architecture. From approximately 1910 onwards, iron cuttings, a by-product of the booming chemical industries, began to be used as a raw material in pigment production. By 1950, the synthetic iron oxide pigments made from iron cuttings had almost completely replaced the natural pigments. However, artists such as Le Corbusier were unwilling to switch from the more luminous burnt Sienna earth pigment to the more opaque and duller synthetic pigments, as long as they could still find suppliers of natural pigments. Saturated, deep brown colors such as 43.4 Terre de Sienne brûlée are manufactured today using complex mixtures that include green and violet pigments.

2 Le Corbusier, *Claviers de Couleurs Salubra 2* (Basel, 1959).
See also Arthur Rüegg (ed.), *Polychromie architecturale. Le Corbusiers Farbenklaviaturen von 1931 und 1959 / Le Corbusier's Color Keyboards from 1931 and 1959 / Les claviers de couleurs de Le Corbusier de 1931 et de 1959* (Basel, Boston, Berlin, 1997) (reprint, 2006).

CMYK approximation:
15.75.80.35

RGB approximation:
130.69.48

Spatial qualities:
dynamic and stable under
all light conditions

Historical pigmentation:
English red

Industrial pigmentation:
red oxide

Facade suitability:
weather-resistant

32.110

Red ocher / Ocre rouge

A shade of Le Corbusier's color palette from 1931[3]

New findings in a cave in Kenya[4] established that red ocher was in use as a
pigment 180,000 years ago, verifying it as one of the world's oldest pigments. It is
the red of ancient architecture in every country and culture. Because there are only
limited supplies of completely formed red earth colors in nature, red ochers were
soon made from yellow ochers by heating them over the fire, or from other compounds
containing iron, such as iron vitriol, by oxidizing and grinding them. Pompeian red,
Indian red, and Persian red were often produced by burning yellow ocher; English red
and caput mortuum were produced almost exclusively by such methods. The name
Red ocher or Ocre rouge, which originally referred only to red earth colors, started
to be used for synthetic products of unknown origin and manufacturing method. This
made it increasingly difficult to differentiate between natural red ochers, pigments
made by heating yellow ochers, or the modern synthetic pigments made from iron
cuttings. Strictly speaking, English red describes a natural ocher that has a slight
yellow tinge. Le Corbusier used the culturally meaningful pigment to color planes
in his architectural conceptions that were meant to advance and be firmly positioned
in space.

3 Le Corbusier, *Claviers de Couleurs Salubra* (Basel, 1931).
  See also Arthur Rüegg (ed.), *Polychromie architecturale. Le Corbusiers Farbenklaviaturen von 1931 und 1959/
  Le Corbusier's Color Keyboards from 1931 and 1959/Les claviers de couleurs de Le Corbusier de 1931 et de 1959*
  (Basel, Boston, Berlin, 1997) (reprint, 2006).
4 Michael Balter, "Human Evolution: Early Start for Human Art? Ochre May Revise Timeline,"
  in *Science*, 5914 (323), 2009, p. 569.

CMYK approximation:
0.45.40.10

RGB approximation:
207.153.127

Spatial qualities:
dynamic and stable under
all light conditions

Historical pigmentation:
English red with chalk

Industrial pigmentation:
red oxide, titanium white,
and umber

Facade suitability:
weather-resistant

32.111

Medium red ocher / Ocre rouge moyen

A shade of Le Corbusier's color palette from 1931[5]

The first Salubra series of 43 monochrome colors was designed for use in architecture. The series includes no less than seven pastel shades made from red earth pigments, among them two pastel shades made from English red, a Le Corbusier favorite which was also included as a full tone color. Le Corbusier felt that the terracotta and salmon shades were particularly useful when striving for an atmosphere of warmth and comfort in his white interiors. The full tone English red described on the previous page is an intense, glowing, earthy-red color that can be lightened beautifully using Champagne chalk, as the color shown here demonstrates. If the space is small and its dimensions are not to be made to appear smaller, then this dynamic nuance should be used on a single, well-lit wall, not on all of them.

5 Le Corbusier, 1931; Rüegg, 1997 (reprint, 2006).

CMYK approximation:
0.20.20.0

RGB approximation:
242.216.296

Spatial qualities:
passive and stable under
all light conditions

Historical pigmentation:
English red with chalk

Industrial pigmentation:
red oxide, titanium white,
and umber

Facade suitability:
weather-resistant

32.112

Light red ocher / Ocre rouge clair

A shade of Le Corbusier's color palette from 1931[6]

Le Corbusier's lightest gradation of English red is a straightforward, down-to-earth color that is light enough to not make a room appear smaller. Adding white to red colors to lighten them is a precarious undertaking, as the countless unpleasant pinks and fleshy colors in fan decks and on facades prove, day in and day out. The older literature for painters mentions pigments such as red bolus that allowed production of particularly attractive light reds: "they are able to create beautiful flesh tones if they are mixed with the appropriate white substrates."[7] Red bolus is a conglomeration of iron oxide, quartz particles, and sand. The secret to mixing lovely pink colors lies in the pigments: the red and white pigments must themselves be luminous and translucent. Flat, unpleasant colors are the result of dull red and flat white pigments that lack the translucency of the quartz particles in red bolus, for instance.

6 Ibid.
7 Translated from Erich Stock,
  Die Grundlagen des Lack- und Farbenfaches, volume IV,
  (Meissen, 1924) p. 63.

CMYK approximation:
40.75.70.40

RGB approximation:
97.59.54

Spatial qualities:
dynamic and stable under
all light conditions

Historical pigmentation:
burnt Sienna earth

Industrial pigmentation:
red oxide, complementary
inorganic pigments

Facade suitability:
weather-resistant

32.120

Brown red / Brun rouge

A shade of Le Corbusier's color palette from 1931[8]

Deeply burnt brown ocher belongs to the spatially effective colors of Le Corbusier's *grande gamme* (major scale). This series was considered to be the most important one for the architect desiring either to create backgrounds rich in atmosphere, or to enhance the three-dimensional effects of the architecture—but not to decorate surfaces or deconstruct space, as Le Corbusier put forth in collaboration with Amédée Ozenfant in an important modernist manifesto entitled "Le Purisme"[9] in 1921.
The art lies in directing the attention of the observer less with intense colors like vermilion (32.090 Rouge foncé or 43.1 Rouge vif), but with muted, burnt ochers, which run little risk of destroying the balance of the spatial composition. Combinations of colors such as Brun rouge with light ultramarines or grays empower and emphasize the reddish-brown painted surface against the more restrained background colors in a room.

8 Le Corbusier, 1981; Rüegg, 1997 (reprint, 2006).
9 Amédée Ozenfant, Charles Edouard-Jeanneret (Le Corbusier),
   "Le Purisme," in *L'Esprit Nouveau* 4 (1921).

CMYK approximation:
10.55.50.20

RGB approximation:
170.118.97

Spatial qualities:
dynamic and stable under
all light conditions

Historical pigmentation:
burnt Sienna earth with chalk

Industrial pigmentation:
red oxide, titanium white and
complementary pigments

Facade suitability:
weather-resistant

32.121

Light brick red / Brique clair

A shade of Le Corbusier's color palette from 1931[10]

Burning the golden yellow earth pigment from Sienna extracts its crystal water, converting the yellowish-brown to a deep red mass of sandy crystals. The depth of color obtained ranges from an orange-brown shade to red depending on the purity of the raw earth pigment that is burnt. The purity and brighter quality of raw Sienna compared to other yellow ochers characterizes burnt Sienna as well; this soon established them as essential pigments for painting and varnishing. "Burnt Sienna possesses shades of such profound depth, that it is astonishing," wrote Erich Stock in 1924.[11] This classic, a strongly muted terra-cotta color, is a derivative of burnt Sienna. Pure burnt Sienna and its pastel shades were omnipresent in Le Corbusier's color concepts, often appearing in combination with grays. Such color combinations are true classics, not a fad of fashion.

10 Le Corbusier, 1931; Rüegg, 1997 (reprint, 2006).
11 Stock, 1924, p. 62.

CMYK approximation:
0.20.35.5

RGB approximation:
232.207.164

Spatial qualities:
passive and stable under
all light conditions

Historical pigmentation:
burnt Sienna earth with chalk

Industrial pigmentation:
red oxide, titanium white and
complementary pigments

Facade suitability:
weather-resistant

32.122

Light native Sienna 2 / Terre de Sienne claire 2

A shade of Le Corbusier's color palette from 1931 [12]

Le Corbusier and Amédée Ozenfant's purist manifesto in *L'Esprit Nouveau* in
1921 described an architectural theory of color, in which colors function as elements
of spatial construction and color subordinates itself to form. Color design should
create a "quiet, anti-dynamic atmosphere," because then, people and their activities
would be the center of attention of life in the architectural space. This architecture
of "humane harmony" [13] called for a palette of strongly grayed colors, in which
the austere, landscape-related pastel shades of natural earth pigments were given
special significance for their ability to warm and soothe. This soft, clay-like
derivative of burnt Sienna earth is light enough to stay in the background and colorful
enough to recall a brick wall bathed in sunlight. This is the color of the dining room
in the Villa La Roche (Le Corbusier, Pierre Jeanneret) in Paris.

12 Le Corbusier, 1931; Rüegg, 1997 (reprint, 2006).
13 John Golding, Christopher Green,
    Léger and Purist Paris (London, 1970), p. 75.

CMYK approximation:
0.10.20.0

RGB approximation:
248.234.207

Spatial qualities:
passive and stable under
all light conditions

Historical pigmentation:
burnt Sienna earth with chalk

Industrial pigmentation:
red oxide, titanium white
and complementary pigments

Facade suitability:
weather-resistant

32.123

Pale native Sienna / Terre de Sienne pâle

A shade of Le Corbusier's color palette from 1931[14]

"Surface colour (a decorative quality) must be used with rigorous discernment to be a natural function of architecture."[15] Fernand Léger wrote this statement in 1924, during a period of groundbreaking technical innovations and new industrial production possibilities that opened the door to the temptation of overdoing color widely. The use of reserved colors made with classic pigments to create color concepts of serenity precludes this ever-present temptation. This flexible, demure, light natural earth shade is also ideal for exterior use. In contrast to colors made from red organic pigments, whose lightened versions look saccharine-sweet and artificial, pastel shades of natural earth pigments retain the grainy, sandy qualities that remind us of the colors found in the landscape.

14 Le Corbusier, 1931; Rüegg, 1997 (reprint, 2006).
15 Fernand Léger, "Polychromatic Architecture," in *L'Architecture Vivante*, autumn/winter 1924, Paris, again in John Golding, Christopher Green (eds.), *Léger and Purist Paris*, London, 1970, p. 95.

CMYK approximation:
60.90.100.40

RGB approximation:
72.40.34

Spatial qualities:
dynamic and stable under all
light conditions

Historical pigmentation:
burnt Sienna earth

Industrial pigmentation:
red oxide and complementary
pigments

Facade suitability:
weather-resistant

26.120

Brown red / Brun rouge

A color in the Villa La Roche by Le Corbusier and Pierre Jeanneret, 1923–1925

The elegant curved ramp in the gallery of the Villa La Roche in Paris has a remarkable history. One color design, for instance, shows the ramp in vermilion red against a moderately saturated ultramarine blue background. However, the ramp was ultimately painted with this luminous, slightly glossy oil paint made with pure burnt Sienna. The wall behind the ramp was confirmed as the background and placed in the shade with velvety gray 32.012 Gris clair 2. Paint layers from later renovations are mute witnesses of the successive flattening of the color brown, caused by the replacement of natural earth pigments and linseed oil with synthetic iron oxide pigments and acrylic binders. The last acrylic coat of paint was correct in its brown hue, but had nothing remotely in common with the depth and luminosity of the original oil paint. In 2009, the villa was repainted with its original colors, thus restoring the ramp to its state of proud grandeur.

The Carmines, Violets, and Purples

The third theme in working with reds is the last one, and also the culmination of them all. The colors in the last two chapters differ in the extent to which they are grayed. This consideration is central in color design, since higher levels of gray in any color increase its effectiveness under conditions of low light, while they decrease its spatial presence. The pure red colors with a tendency towards yellow presented in chapter 8, the erotic red vermilion shades, are most beautiful when placed in the light. The general tendency of reds to mark their presence in space, to make objects appear larger, and make surfaces seem to advance, are most powerful with the vermilion reds, but these effects lose their dominance as these red colors are muted by adding white. The rather gray, reddish-brown colors and their lighter pastel shades described in chapter 9 have, in fact, already sacrificed some of the fiery reds' tendency to expand and to dominate; they have not, however, lost their ability to stabilize and fix the plane in space.

The following focuses on the bluish reds, from carmine and ruby to magenta and violet. Increasing the proportion of blue in colors generally allows them to become cooler and appear more distant. The higher blue content allows them to remain beautiful in the shade, as does a higher gray content. The higher blue content, however, also allows colors to retreat in space, an effect not observed with added gray. Applied to reds, this means that adding blue will make them more resistant to changes in the light, will stabilize them in the shade, and will cause them to advance less forcefully in space.

Chapter 8 described the warm red scale, this chapter presents the shades of the cool red color scale. This differentiation between warm and cool is unusual compared to standard practice. Its significance with respect to color design is the topic of the next chapter's introduction. The following thoughts address the method for mixing pastels, because it is particularly difficult to produce pleasant pink nuances when lightening colors such as carmine red, aubergine, or magenta. "The lighter shades of color are usually adjusted by adding a small amount of the next more intensive shade, so as to mask their

"Ruby red: Similar [in color] to the precious stone, which consists principally of aluminum oxide coloured with small quantities of hematite and chromiumoxide. An Eastern legend, however, claims that the color originated as the blood of a queen spilled on a diamond and created the ruby; it must have been a queen with 'blue blood' in her veins."
A. Kornerup and J.H. Wanscher, 1961 [1]

tendency to become visibly dull upon adding white. [...] In contrast, some shades, especially those that contain large quantities of synthetic organic pigments, display the opposite inclination. This is usually adjusted by adding an equally light, gray color." Otto Prase,[2] who wrote these lines and was rumored to be a gifted master of painting, a teacher and theorist, devised a little-known color system[3] called *Baumanns Neue Farbtonkarten System Prase*. It was published in 1912 and remained on the market for several decades. This color system is unique because each one of the nearly 1300 samples on the color cards includes its own formula of pigments. The pigments to be mixed to produce the darkest shade of a dark-to-light progression of colors are listed first. This could be, for instance, a regal deep purple which progresses through three medium dark shades to end with a tender pink. The formulae for the lighter pastel shades are given in terms of the amount of the dark shade plus the appropriate amount of a white. It is standard practice today to lighten all paints with titanium white; the Baumann Prase color card formulae made use of a number of white pigments. Red colors with a bluish hue were lightened with translucent zinc white; reds with gray content or a yellow hue were lightened with opaque chalk.

The addition of gray adjusted to the desired degree of lightness was used to curb the artificial, intrusive quality of pinks often obtained when mixing pigments other than natural reds and whites.

Examining the color cards reveals that this forgotten realm of highly different-iated knowledge concerning pigments and pigment mixtures produced astonishingly beautiful colors, color card by color card. There are no inexpressive, intrusive, or dull shades within them.

The beauty of the many pastel shades in Le Corbusier's collection of mono-chrome wallpapers for the Salubra company implies that the renowned wallpaper manufacturer lightened darker colors with gray as well. In the process of reconstructing Le Corbusier's 1931 polychromy, the dullness caused by adding white had to be corrected by adding more of the complementary color (green to red, orange to blue, red to green), in order to achieve the desired depth of color.

---

1 Translated from Andreas Kornerup and Johann W. Wanscher, *Taschenlexikon der Farben* (Kopenhagen 1961, Göttingen 1963, 3rd ed. 1981), p. 195.
2 Translated from Otto Prase, *Baumanns Neue Farbtonkarten System Prase* (Aue / Saxony, 1928).
3 See Werner Spillmann, *Farb-Systeme 1611–2007* (Basel, 2009), p. 104.

CMYK approximation:
70.90.75.0

RGB approximation:
94.57.71

Spatial qualities:
dynamic

Historical pigmentation:
caput mortuum and ultra-
marine blue

Industrial pigmentation:
red oxide deep and complementary pigments

Facade suitability:
weather-resistant in some
techniques

43.26

Aubergine / Aubergine

Hans Kittel, color card in the book *Pigmente*, 1960 [4]

Converting iron vitriol into sulfuric acid creates a dark brownish-violet pigment that was not well-liked initially. It was thus given the name caput mortuum, which in Latin means dead head or worthless remains. The morbid name is not a reference to the toxicity of the pigment, because it, like all other iron oxides, is entirely non-toxic—it was meant to describe a disappointing color. Good news followed in 1918: "It has recently been learned that very beautiful and fiery colors can be made out of this inferior by-product. They are now an important product for trade." [5] They have remained so to this day. Caput mortuum and its derivative colors, such as Aubergine, have since enjoyed great popularity. They have provided architects with a contained, noble color that forfeits nothing of its beauty irrespective of the ambient lighting, which may be neutral or cause Aubergine to shift towards brown or blue.

4 Hans Kittel, *Pigmente. Herstellung, Eigenschaften, Anwendung*
(Stuttgart, 1960), in the appendix.
5 Josef Bersch, *Die Fabrikation der Erdfarben*
(Vienna, Leipzig, [3]1918), p. 178.

CMYK approximation:
40.70.20.20

RGB approximation:
126.82.114

Spatial qualities:
dynamic

Historical pigmentation:
ultramarine blue and
rose madder or alizarin
crimson

Industrial pigmentation:
complex mixtures of organic
and inorganic pigments

Facade suitability:
not weather-resistant

07.055

Loos' violet / Violet Loos

Adolf Loos, color of a Salubra wallpaper in the Villa Müller, 1930

In 1930 Adolf Loos used a Salubra wallpaper coated with madder lake and
ultramarine blue in the Villa Müller in Prague. Cennino Cennini had already noted in
the late Middle Ages that a beautiful violet could be produced using equal parts
of rose madder and ultramarine blue pigments.[6] Mixing these two venerated, rather
transparent pigments with chalk to create a beautiful, spatially withdrawn violet
was nothing new. What came as a surprise was that Adolf Loos, a self-declared oppo-
nent of "useless" decoration, used Salubra wallpaper in the Villa Müller and,
then, in a color that could polarize and provoke like few others. Violets are sensitive
to changes in light and quickly shift to brown. The ultramarine blue content in
Loos' violet minimizes this risk.

6 Cennino d'Andrea Cennini, *The Craftsman's Handbook «Il Libro dell'Arte»*
(New York, 1954), p. 52.

CMYK approximation:
25.60.20.10

RGB approximation:
163.113.135

Spatial qualities:
dynamic

Historical pigmentation:
ultramarine blue, alizarin
crimson, chalk

Industrial pigmentation:
complex mixtures of organic
and inorganic pigments

Facade suitability:
not weather-resistant

08.008

Matt lilac / Lilas mate

Lightened version of 07.055 Loos Violet, 2008

Viewing the pigment (the colorant as a material), color perception (the physiology), and color meaning (an individual and collective act of assessment) as separate realms of knowledge is a phenomenon of the twentieth century. Color perception based on light and not on pigments became the major area of interest, and this led to greater ease in handling and in communication. Like any categorization, this division involved separation and reduction. Inherent to any act of reductionism is the danger that information outside the new realm of knowledge will get lost. With regard to color and color usage, a treasure of empirical knowledge accumulated over thousands of years about pigments and their specific effects. The aspect of color meaning as it relates to specific coloring materials was neglected and, finally, forgotten. Historic literature can be very helpful. It tells us that lilac, the lightened version of a bluish, "excellent and beautiful" violet made from ultramarine blue and pinkish rose madder, works particularly well placed in shadow.[7] The high ultramarine content protects Matt lilac against the light sensitivity of lilacs made using other formulae.

7 George Field, *The Rudiments of Colour and Colouring*
(London, 1870), p. 139.

CMYK approximation:
40.90.60.30
RGB approximation:
105.43.62

Spatial qualities:
dynamic, festive even
in shadow

Historical pigmentation:
cadmium red dark

Industrial pigmentation:
DPP ruby with umber

Facade suitability:
weather-resistant in some
techniques

43.12

Ruby red / Rouge rubis

A shade of Le Corbusier's color palette from 1959[8]

Wittgenstein noted, in his philosophical remarks on colors and on the logic of color notions, that "dark red" and "blackish red" are not equal, because on inspection a ruby can still look dark red, but, if it is transparent, it does not look blackish-red. While black seems to mute a color and increase its opacity, darkness, however, only mutes, continues the philosopher.[9] Equating black with an absolute muting quality, and darkness with a transparent one, parallels the effects observable when mixing pigments. Adding black to a red color will negate the Ruby red pigment's luminosity, while adding a complementary green actually produces a luminous, darker shade of the same red. Using a formula that produces a color that is as matt as possible will result in a velvety, Ruby red color surface that is festive and luxurious.

8 Le Corbusier, *Claviers de Couleurs Salubra 2* (Basel, 1959).
   See also Arthur Rüegg (ed.), *Polychromie architecturale. Le Corbusiers Farbenklaviaturen von 1931 und 1959 / Le Corbusier's Color Keyboards from 1931 and 1959 / Les claviers de couleurs de Le Corbusier de 1931 et de 1959* (Basel, Boston, Berlin, 1997) (reprint, 2006).
9 Translated from Ludwig Wittgenstein, *Bemerkungen über die Farben* (Frankfurt, 1974), p. 80, 109.

CMYK approximation:
0.95.50.45

RGB approximation:
121.16.52

Spatial qualities:
dynamic, effective even
in shadow

Historical pigmentation:
cochineal, later thioindigo
red

Industrial pigmentation:
organic red pigments

Facade suitability:
not weather-resistant

32.100

Carmine red / Rouge carminé

A shade of Le Corbusier's color palette from 1931[10]

The dried bodies of the female kermes and cochineal insects produce a uniquely transparent, eminently treasured, deep red color. Cochineal insect cultures were already in existence when the Spanish conquered Mexico. Erich Stock writes, that "half a million animals were killed" to produce one kilo of dried cochineal.[11] The color Carmine red "conveys an impression of gravity and dignity and at the same time of grace and attractiveness" (Goethe).[12] In 1467, when the Ottoman wars brought the trade in Tyrian purple to a standstill, representatives of the church declared that Carmine red should succeed the pigment from the conch as the new divine color. Together with its more lightfast, synthetically produced successors, such as carminic acid, the luminous bluish-red pigment is unique among all the sources of brilliant red colors. Le Corbusier appreciated transparent pigments such as carmine for their ability to decorate surfaces. In contrast to opaque reds, which lend weight to the plane or an object, transparent, deep reds do not bond with the object; they remain a quality of the surface. Rouge carminé decorates it and looks noble, even under low light.

10 Le Corbusier, *Claviers de Couleurs Salubra* (Basel, 1931).
    See also Arthur Rüegg (ed.), *Polychromie architecturale. Le Corbusiers Farbenklaviaturen von 1931 und 1959 / Le Corbusier's Color Keyboards from 1931 and 1959 / Les claviers de couleurs de Le Corbusier de 1931 et de 1959* (Basel, Boston, Berlin, 1997) (reprint, 2006).
11 Erich Stock, *Das Buch der Farben* (Göttingen, ²1956), p. 245.
12 Johann Wolfgang von Goethe, *Theory of Colours* (London, 1840), section 796, p. 314.

CMYK approximation:
0.100.35.35

RGB approximation:
137.0.66

Spatial qualities:
dynamic, effective even
in shadow

Historical pigmentation:
alizarin, iron salt

Industrial pigmentation:
organic red pigments

Facade suitability:
not weather-resistant

32.101

Raspberry red / Rouge framboise

A shade of Le Corbusier's color palette from 1931[13]

The root of the rubia tinctorum, or madder root, has been known as a coloring
agent since ancient times. The madder root contains various, anthraquinone derived
coloring substances, principally ruberythric acid, alizarin, purpurin, and pseudo-
purpurin. The shades vary from scarlet to red with a bluish tint. The red pigments
obtained from the root were so sought after that worldwide production levels
rose to 70,000 metric tons, with a value of 70 million marks![14] By the late nineteenth
century, however, the individual colorants could be synthesized industrially, allowing
specific production of the most valued shades available from the hydroxyanthra-
quinone base. The color can be made to vary from deep violet to rose, depending on
the structure of the pigment and on the inorganic substrate, iron salts shifting
the hue towards violet, alum towards crimson. They are surpassed in brilliance only
by the true, insect carmines (cf. page 220). Le Corbusier's Rouge framboise is part
of the decorative palette of colors, being rather transparent and a quality of
the surface, not of the volume.

13 Le Corbusier, 1931; Rüegg, 1997 (reprint, 2006).
14 Erich Stock, *Die Grundlagen des Lack- und Farbenfaches, volume IV*
(Meissen, 1924), p. 143.

CMYK approximation:
0.30.30.5

RGB approximation:
226.188.162

Spatial qualities:
dynamic, effective even
in shadow

Historical pigmentation:
alizarin, iron salt with zinc
white

Industrial pigmentation:
organic red pigments, cobalt
green, yellow oxide

Facade suitability:
not weather-resistant

32.102

Pale pink / Rose pâle

A shade of Le Corbusier's color palette from 1931[15]

The sequence of numbers in the first Salubra series indicates the base pigment.
The thoughtful numbering system is logical from the first to the last shade.
Le Corbusier used the same number scheme in his list of paints for the Frugès housing
estate in Pessac. It included, for instance, a color 130 ("terre d'ombre brûlée"),
which corresponds to Salubra shade 32.130, also a dark, burnt umber; color 91 ("rouge
vermillon + blanc, un vermillon solide de commerce"), corresponds to Salubra shade
32.091, a lightened version of synthetic vermilion pigment. This straightforward
numbering systematization is based on the pigment. Thus, 32.102 Pale pink is a lighter
version of the previous color 32.101 Rouge framboise; both are made with synthetic
madder lake, one is the full tone, the other a pastel. Zinc white was used to lighten the
red, thereby preventing the splendid red pigment from turning into a saccharine-
sweet, unnatural pink, since zinc white creates luminous, slightly bluish nuances. It is
advisable today to counter the overbearing effect of titanium white by adding chrome
green and yellow oxide.

---

15 Le Corbusier, 1931; Rüegg, 1997 (reprint, 2006).

CMYK approximation:
0.50.10.5

RGB approximation:
215.151.166

Spatial qualities:
dynamic

Historical pigmentation:
most likely a synthetic
organic carmine pigment

Industrial pigmentation:
complex pigment mixture
and white

Facade suitability:
not weather-resistant

43.3

Pink / Rose

A shade of Le Corbusier's color palette from 1959 [16]

In the early years of his creative practice, Le Corbusier used austere pinks made from natural earth pigments. His strict avoidance of unnatural-looking colors would later soften. This pink color can only be formulated with synthetic red pigments. We have not heard of nor seen this pink used by Le Corbusier on a surface in his architecture, yet Rose does appear in tapestries, paintings, and sculptures he created, often combined with 43.20 Jaune vif, 43.1 Rouge vif, and 43.7 Vert vif. The color 43.3 Rose together with 43.13 Bleu ceruleum also creates an idiosyncratic, balanced color combination. Because Le Corbusier's use of color in the 1950s focused on balancing his architectural compositions by means of isolated elements of color, colors tended to be paired, and not used singly. It is safe to assume that he considered Rose as an important complement to other saturated colors.

16 Le Corbusier, 1959; Rüegg, 1997 (reprint, 2006).

CMYK approximation:
20.100.0.10

RGB approximation:
152.0.110

Spatial qualities:
dynamic, luminous also in
shadow

Historical pigmentation:
brilliant pink and shell limestone

Industrial pigmentation:
magenta with chalk

Facade suitability:
not weather-resistant

06.001

Hot Magenta / Magenta avide

Michael Dax, architect, 2003, after Luis Barragán

Luis Barragán devoted himself to architecture that he understood to be "a sublime act of poetic imagination."[17] This is evident in Barragán's choice of color and in his concepts, with their convincing interplay of color and light. Inspired during a stay in Mexico, exhibition architect Michael Dax was looking for a specific Barragán pink for his residence. From the many hues offered, he selected 06.001 Hot magenta. The extraordinarily luminous color is based on an industrially manufactured pigment, quinacridone magenta, which was first produced in 1955. The more recent invention of the quinacridone pigment precluded the use of this particular pink in 1940 in the atelier house he built for the painter José Clemente Orozco. He may have used "Brilliant pink," the trade name for a pigment available at the time of construction, which was not as lightfast, but similar in color, and similar in its ability to bathe a room in gentle, pink light. It is advisable to adjust the color with a transparent white such as lime or chalk, because adding titanium white will obscure the luminous, nanoscale particles of magenta.

17 Luis Barragán, Laureate Acceptance Speech, 1980,
  see http://www.pritzkerprize.com/laureates/1980/_downloads/1980_Acceptance_Speech.pdf.

CMYK approximation:
75.70.10.0

RGB approximation:
96.84.144

Spatial qualities:
dynamic

Historical pigmentation:
ultramarine violet

Industrial pigmentation:
ultramarine violet

Facade suitability:
not weather-resistant

06.029

Ultramarine violet / Outremer violet

Hans Kittel, color card in the book *Pigmente*, 1960 [18]

Johannes Itten wrote that the mysterious color of violet could only be understood
by the heart.[19] Le Corbusier avoided using violet as a wall color, stating that it would
create unpleasant vibrations in architectural space. Statements such as these
display a high level of ambivalence, and can be explained in part by the fact that violet
colors display two absorption maxima in their interaction with light. Depending on
the spectral distribution of light, either the blue maximum can dominate, making the
same color appear cool and melancholic, or the red maximum can dominate, which makes
it appear brown. Ultramarine violet is less prone to shift than other colors, because
blue dominates throughout. Nonetheless it is advisable to use such shades on one surface only. If used on more surfaces, reflections will intensify the spatial ambivalence
of violet, creating an unpredictable space, light and color drama.

18 Kittel, 1960.
19 See Klausbernd Vollmar, *Farben. Symbolik – Wirkung – Deutung*
(Munich, 2009), p. 176.

CMYK approximation:
30.80.0.0

RGB approximation:
161.77.143

Spatial qualities:
dynamic and mysterious
in shadow

Historical pigmentation:
a pink pigment that is
not lightfast and no longer
available

Industrial pigmentation:
fluorescent pink and marble
powder

Facade suitability:
not weather-resistant

08.067

Purple rose YK / Rose Yves Klein

Yves Klein, artist, 1960

Yves Klein began in 1949 to experiment with monochrome painting; he would later sign his famous blue surfaces with "Yves le Monochrome." Klein is mainly associated with his works in ultramarine blue, but beginning in 1960, he increasingly used a trinity of pigments for his later works: ultramarine blue, the immaterial; pink, the embodiment; and gold, which connects the two, the enlightenment. In 1959, Klein wrote about the equivalence of these three colors. In the trinity, pink represents the material side of the visible world, temptation, and the source of all creative impulses. Ultramarine blue overcomes the material world and marks the transition to the immaterial. Gold connects the two and represents both perfection and that which is unattainable. Klein wrote that pink, literally and metaphorically, clarifies and reinforces the sense of the blue.[20] 08.067 Purple rose YK is made with the pigment mix used by the Yves Klein Foundation for Yves Klein installations and objects.

20 Centre Pompidou, *Yves Klein. Body, Colour, Immaterial*, exhibition from October 5, 2006 till February 5, 2007, description on the internet: http://www.centrepompidou.fr/education/ressources/ENS-klein-EN/ENS-klein-EN.htm (accessed 16.11.09).

The Blues

Blue is by far the most beloved color of all, as Eva Heller writes; very few people dislike blue.[2] The most common associations are the sky and water.[3] *"Blue is the quintessential color of the sky.* Blue is profound in the way it creates an essence of calmness. When blue sinks towards black, it has overtones of other-worldly mourning," wrote Kandinsky in his famous book on the means of art[4]

"As the upper sky and distant mountains appear blue, so a blue surface seems to retire from us. But as we readily follow an agreeable object that flies from us, so we love to contemplate blue, not because it advances to us, but because it draws us after it.
When blue partakes in some degree of the *plus* side [yellow, reddish yellow, yellowish red], the effect is not disagreeable. Sea-green is a rather pleasing color."
Johann Wolfgang von Goethe[1]

and extends the blue arc from sky to calmness, melancholy, and mourning. Le Corbusier also speaks of two different atmospheric effects of blue in the architectural context: he classifies colors made with ultramarine blue as those with an effect of infinite quietude, and those made with the slightly greenish pigments cerulean blue and ultramarine green, as giving the impression of the more perceptible dimensions of the sky and sea. With these ideas and other artistic practices in mind, dividing the blue nuances into two groups is useful for the design practice. The specific pigments, their physical properties, and cultural implications, and not the position on the color wheel, determine how they can best be used to define space. Omitting the cultural background is particularly misleading in dealing with the sky blues, because the specific effect of a blue is largely influenced by the pigment it is made from. Goethe had the dark blue, transparent indigo pigment at his disposal, and his statements concerning the proximity of black to blue gain a new meaning when this is considered. When Yves Klein said "blue," he meant ultramarine blue, and this descriptive precision is essential when interpreting his positions.

Statements about the potential effects of colors in space are most convincing when based on a mixture of colorimetry and the broadest possible, intersubjective evaluation of its meaning, as *well* as the chemistry of the pigment used.

The first group of blue nuances contains paints made from the chemically similar sulfur pigments, natural lapis lazuli and synthetic ultramarine blue. Lapis lazuli is created by volcanic activity in nature, and ultramarine blue under controlled conditions from colorless minerals in the furnace. Both pigments contain a $[S^3]^{2-}$-ion. The most expensive and bluest lapis lazuli semi-precious stones contain more of these ions than less valuable examples, because the sulfur particles are what produces the pigment's blue color. The unique sulfur chemistry allows ultramarine blue and lapis lazuli to appear remarkably blue even in shadow. The transition undergone by the sulfur ions is dissimilar from other pigments' physical interactions with light leading to blue color, which is why it is necessary to create a completely separate category for these blues. "What is blue? Blue is the invisible becoming visible," wrote Yves Klein—he was referring exclusively to ultramarine blue.[5]

The second group of blue nuances includes colors made from pigments with green content, such as cerulean, Prussian, or phthalocyanine blue. Picasso's melancholic paintings from his blue period would not have been possible without the almost black Prussian blue and its dense, opaque pastel shades. Cobalt and cerulean blue pigments produce more substantial blue colors than the escapist shades made with ultramarine blue. Lightened shades of these colors are warmer and more tangible, as are all blue colors with a green content. This means that two equally light blue nuances, but with a difference in their content of green, will exhibit spatial differences. A pastel hue made from ultramarine blue will appear more immaterial and airy. This will increase the perceived distance between the surface and the viewer the most. A light color made from Prussian, cerulean, or phthalocyanine blue will appear to be more substantial and escape less.

1 Johann Wolfgang von Goethe, *Theory of Colours* (London, 1840),
   sections 780, 781, 785, p. 311, 312
2 Translated from Eva Heller, *Wie Farben wirken.*
   Farbpsychologie, Farbsymbolik, kreative Farbgestaltung (Reinbek near Hamburg, 1999), p. 23.
3 Translated from Ingrid Riedel, *Farben in Religion, Gesellschaft, Kunst und Psychotherapie,*
   (Stuttgart, 1999), p. 58.
4 Translated from Wassily Kandinsky, *Über das Geistige in der Kunst* (Bern, 1952)
   (German original edition, 1910).
5 Philip Ball, *Bright Earth. Art and the Invention of Colour* (New York, 2001), p. 231

Pantone approximation:
PM Reflex Blue

CMYK approximation:
100.80.0.40

RGB approximation:
38.41.94

Spatial qualities:
dynamic, convincing even
in the shade

Historical pigmentation:
ultramarine blue, ivory black,
zinc white

Industrial pigmentation:
ultramarine blue, phthalocyanine blue, oxide pigments

Facade suitability:
not weather-resistant

43.18

Deep blue / Bleu foncé

A shade of Le Corbusier's color palette from 1959[6]

When our attempts failed to convert Prussian blue into the deep, sensual blue shown here, we turned to a recipe from an old textbook on painting. This dark blue is sensational as a deeply matt, glue-based paint. The extreme transparency of blue pigments, such as indigo, Prussian blue, ultramarine blue, or cobalt blue, makes them particularly sensitive to additional pigments. Before the advent of the paint industries, "color" factories produced pigments, not paints, and painters mixed pigments with binders themselves. Their handbooks were filled with helpful information. A beautiful dark blue is created by adding ivory black and a small amount of zinc white to ultramarine blue. Ultramarine blue, otherwise used to blacken less black pigments, turns into a deep, powdery, matt blue shade when mixed with the velvety ivory black. It creates a color that calls to mind a dusky song, or the idea of infinity. No other pigment mixtures will achieve the same depth of hue, matt surface, and outstanding opacity.

6 Le Corbusier, *Claviers de Couleurs Salubra 2* (Basel, 1959).
See also Arthur Rüegg (ed.), *Polychromie architecturale. Le Corbusiers Farbenklaviaturen von 1931 und 1959 / Le Corbusier's Color Keyboards from 1931 and 1959 / Les claviers de couleurs de Le Corbusier de 1931 et de 1959* (Basel, Boston, Berlin, 1997) (reprint, 2006).

Pantone approximation:
PM 072

CMYK approximation:
100.100.0.0

RGB approximation:
56.23.120

Spatial qualities:
dynamic, luminous even in
the shade

Historical pigmentation:
pure ultramarine blue

Industrial pigmentation:
pure ultramarine blue

Facade suitability:
not weather-resistant

03.001

Ultramarine blue YK / Bleu outremer Yves Klein

Yves Klein, artist, 1957

When Yves Klein chose ultramarine blue for his monochrome paintings, he situated himself within the tradition of medieval color symbolism, which believed that lapis lazuli blue (natural ultramarine blue) embodied the transcendent and the infinite.[7] "The recipe [for which a patent was requested but not granted] may now be divulged, yet the secret of this color remains. A phenomenon is observed again and again by almost everyone that has voiced an opinion, thus, one may begin to speak of an objective, or better yet: an intersubjective definition: and this is the double nature of the color that as a powder possesses material and haptic qualities, but upon closer observation, the material dissolves into its own opposite and recedes into a profound depth. This process of transformation effects the transcendence of this color and explains its magic."[8] Magic indeed, and a fascination that can lead to an excess! On individual surfaces, on large canvases, and in spaces of concentration, this powerful blue can hardly fail to leave its impression.

7 Translated from *Beate Epperlein, Monochrome Malerei* (Nuremberg, 1997), p. 89.
8 Translated from Hans Gercke (ed.), *Blau – Farbe der Ferne* (Heidelberg, 1990), p. 426–427.

Pantone approximation:
90.80.0.10

RGB approximation:
65.57.128

Spatial qualities:
dynamic, luminous even in
the shade

Historical pigmentation:
--

Industrial pigmentation:
ultramarine blue with cobalt
blue

Facade suitability:
weather-resistant if acid-
stabilized ultramarine
is used

09.011

Deep ultramarine blue / Bleu outremer sombre

Created for André Heller in 2004 as the best approximation of Yves Klein blue as an enamel paint

The extremely high price of natural ultramarine (lapis lazuli) quickly triggered
a desire to develop a less expensive industrial version. In 1797, Goethe pointed out
that a blue deposit in lime kilns was similar in color to lapis lazuli. In 1828,
three scientists almost concurrently described methods to synthesize the desired
color by heating china clay (kaolin), lime, and sodium sulphate. In 1828, Jean Baptiste
Guimet was awarded the "Société d'Encouragement" prize of 6,000 francs for the
development of a method to synthetically produce ultramarine. This was the beginning
of the incomparably beautiful, blue pigment's triumphal procession around the
world. Ultramarine blue reacts sensitively to binders, it is dark and transparent in
acrylic and oil techniques, but mixing it with pure cobalt blue can reduce its
transparency and create a deep blue color that differs enough from the powdery matt
blue of ultramarine in glue-based techniques to give it a different color name.

Pantone approximation:
PM 286

CMYK approximation:
80.60.0.10

RGB approximation:
83.90.151

Spatial qualities:
dynamic, luminous even in
the shade

Historical pigmentation:
ultramarine blue, slightly
grayed

Industrial pigmentation:
ultramarine blue, slightly
grayed

Facade suitability:
not weather-resistant

43.10

Ultramarine blue 1959 / Bleu outremer 1959

A shade of Le Corbusier's color palette from 1959 [9]

"Azzuro oltremarino is most likely a very treasured color, its beauty surpasses all other colors," [10] wrote the Florentine Cennino d'Andrea Cennini in a medieval handbook for painters, which not only explains the spectacular handling of color in the Middle Ages, but also tells of a proud artisan craft. The fascination with ultramarine blue is universal: Yves Klein was mentioned above, but Le Corbusier also valued the pigment. In his series of architecturally significant colors selected for their effectiveness in modulating space, seven ultramarines were included among the 63 nuances. Light ultramarine nuances elude attention; they blend with the sky or with our thoughts about the sky. Dark ultramarines such as this are perceived more as a spectacle. They transcend intellectual categorization.

9 Le Corbusier, 1959; Rüegg, 1997 (reprint, 2006).
10 Translated from *Das Buch von der Kunst oder Traktat der Malerei des Cennino Cennini da Colle di Valdelsa*, translated, with introduction, notes and register provided by Albert Ilg (Vienna, 1871), p. 37.

CMYK approximation:
45.10.0.10

RGB approximation:
154.179.212

Spatial qualities:
dynamic

Historical pigmentation:
Cobalt-cerulean blue with
zinc white

Industrial pigmentation:
cobalt blue, red oxide, and
titanium white

Facade suitability:
weather-resistant in some
techniques

43.13

Cerulean blue / Bleu ceruleum

A shade of Le Corbusier's color palette from 1959 [11]

This nuance from the later palette is derived from cerulean blue. It is denser, scarcely grayed, and more spatially present than Le Corbusier's preferred cerulean blue colors in the purist era, such as 32.030 Bleu ceruleum foncé. The pigment and color name is derived from the Latin word for sky (caeruleum), a name that later was used for the expensive, cobalt blue pigment. The difference seen here—between the darker and less luminous color of the earlier palette, whose nuances unfolded against a white background, and were meant to create atmosphere, and the more brilliant color of the later scale, whose nuances were to be noticeable in large spaces as a means of contrast against dark backgrounds—is typical of Le Corbusier's development. Color 43.13 Bleu ceruleum has the same simultaneous red and green tinge as the blue of the sky, and it can be combined with almost any other color.

11 Le Corbusier, 1959; Rüegg, 1997 (reprint, 2006).

Pantone approximation:
PM 2718

RGB approximation:
119.127.175

Spatial qualities:
dynamic, luminous even in
the shade

Historical pigmentation:
ultramarine blue with zinc
white

Industrial pigmentation:
ultramarine blue with titanium
white and violet

Facade suitability:
weather-resistant in some
techniques

32.020

Ultramarine blue 1931 / Bleu outremer 1931

A shade of Le Corbusier's color palette from 1931[12]

The Salubra wallpaper collection published 1931 was constructed systematically
using hues designed to heighten the three-dimensional effects of purist architecture.
The palette was composed so as to allow the most important colors of the palette,
a group of calm, background nuances made with various pigments, to be complemented
with a second group of more dynamic, stronger colors. The ultramarine blue described
here belonged to this dynamic group. Since all of the color shades in the palette
were designed to balance each other and ensure ready combinations, Le Corbusier
moderated the otherwise overpowering ultramarine pigment with zinc white. This
created an ultramarine blue that was less captivating than the purer and darker ultramarines without hampering its ability to be wonderfully effective in conditions of
low light.

12 Le Corbusier, *Claviers de Couleurs Salubra* (Basel 1931).
    See also Arthur Rüegg (ed.), *Polychromie architecturale. Le Corbusiers Farbenklaviaturen von 1931 und 1959 /*
    Le Corbusier's Color Keyboards from 1931 and 1959 / Les claviers de couleurs de Le Corbusier de 1931 et de 1959
    (Basel, Boston, Berlin, 1997) (reprint 2006).

CMYK approximation:
35.10.0.10

RGB approximation:
171.188.215

Spatial qualities:
dynamic, luminous even in
the shade

Historical pigmentation:
ultramarine blue with zinc
white

Industrial pigmentation:
ultramarine blue with titanium
white and iron oxide

Facade suitability:
weather-resistant in some
techniques

32.021

Sky blue / Bleu ciel

A shade of Le Corbusier's color palette from 1931 [13]

In a unique attempt to introduce a system to the world of imaginative color
names in the 1960s, Kornerup and Wanscher first categorized color names, such
as sky blue, alphabetically and then related them to numbered color fields. Blue ciel
or Sky blue, the color in this example, corresponds to the color field numbered
22 A5. Unfortunately, not all color fields have a colloquial name because the termino-
logical specification is based on known color terms and color meaning, not on
science. Sky blue is the color "of a cloudless sky on a sunny summer day at about
midday, viewed from an angle of approximately 30°." [14] Clear, cheerful lightened
versions of ultramarine blue, such as this, provided painters with a sunlit sky blue.
In contrast, lightened versions of Prussian blue create more gloomy sky blues,
such as those used by Picasso during his blue period.

13 Ibid.
14 Andreas Kornerup and Johann H. Wanscher,
   Taschenlexikon der Farben
   (Zurich, Göttingen, 1961), p. 174.

CMYK approximation:
30.10.10.0

RGB approximation:
195.207.217

Spatial qualities:
passive, particularly beautiful in the shade

Historical pigmentation:
ultramarine blue with chalk and umber

Industrial pigmentation:
ultramarine blue with titanium white and oxide pigments

Facade suitability:
weather-resistant

32.022

Medium ultramarine / Bleu outremer moyen

A shade of Le Corbusier's color palette from 1931[15]

The light-to-dark scale of ultramarine blue composed by Le Corbusier begins with 32.020 Bleu outremer 1931 and ends with 32.024 Bleu pâle. The second lighter version of ultramarine blue marks the transition from the dynamic ultramarines to the background colors that are more passive and stabilize themselves in space. Small spaces can be optically widened using these ultramarine shades, and dark spaces can be made to seem less gloomy. This color along with the next three is especially effective when applied to surfaces that have little light. Le Corbusier liked to combine surfaces painted with dark, burnt earth tones such as 32.120 Brun rouge or 32.130 Marron with those painted with light shades of ultramarine. This positioned the brown-red elements in space and allowed the blue-gray surfaces to recede to the background as a matter of course—a method of combining colors as effective as it ever was.

15 Le Corbusier, 1931; Rüegg, 1997 (reprint, 2006).

CMYK approximation:
25.10.10.0

RGB approximation:
204.212.218

Spatial qualities:
passive, particularly beautiful in the shade

Historical pigmentation:
ultramarine blue with chalk and umber

Industrial pigmentation:
ultramarine blue with titanium white and oxide pigments

Facade suitability:
weather-resistant

32.023

Light blue / Bleu clair

A shade of Le Corbusier's color palette from 1931 [16]

The chemistry of the ultramarine blue pigment lends the pigment a unique presence in low light conditions. Ultramarine pigments absorb high-frequency waves and transform this energy into a wavelength that we perceive as the color blue. Consequently, colors that contain even small amounts of ultramarine blue already display a remarkable beauty and a reliable, receding quality. Because little light is needed to create a visibly blue color, it is advisable to paint large surfaces with a color slightly lighter than that chosen based on small color examples. This ability to make much blue with little light gives ultramarine blue a special place among the pigments, and it reveals why ultramarine cannot be replaced by other blue pigments.

16 Le Corbusier, 1959; Rüegg, 1997 (reprint, 2006).

CMYK approximation:
10.3.10.0

RGB approximation:
235.238.230

Spatial qualities:
passive, particularly beautiful in the shade

Historical pigmentation:
ultramarine blue with chalk and natural umber

Industrial pigmentation:
titanium white, cobalt blue, and oxide pigments

Facade suitability:
weather-resistant

32.024

Pale blue / Bleu pâle

A shade of Le Corbusier's color palette from 1931[17]

Is this a blue color or a gray? Bleu pâle mixes sky blue with shadow gray. It is a color that poses a question without providing a clear answer. Because it dictates no answer and leaves room for different interpretations, this color (and other either-or colors) lends wings to our imagination. This is the lightest ultramarine shade in Le Corbusier's palette. Simple lightened versions of ultramarine blue are airy and clearly light blue. Lightened versions of natural umber are shady and earthy-gray. When combined, air and shadow, or the earth and the sky, approach each other. This intentional combination is what makes this color appealing. Bleu pâle recedes and unfolds its strikingly ambiguous effect most beautifully in the shade.

17 Ibid.

CMYK approximation:
40.20.15.5

RGB approximation:
165.175.190

Spatial qualities:
dynamic, also beautiful in
the shade

Historical pigmentation:
ultramarine blue with chalk,
red ocher, and umber

Industrial pigmentation:
ultramarine blue with titanium
white and oxide pigments

Facade suitability:
weather-resistant in some
techniques

32.021 S

Salubra 1997 / Salubra 1997

Arthur Rüegg, architect, 1997

The first edition of Arthur Rüegg's 1997 book, *Polychromie architecturale*,[18] shows a sky blue that is significantly grayer than the one shown in the second edition.[19] The gray tint of the first Salubra reprint is a result of the fact that the wallpaper samples from 1931 vary in color, some of them being browner, others in a better state of conservation. Thus, the reprint reflects to some extent the state of the sample used to mix the paint. The color is unique because it reacts so clearly to light changes throughout the day, without being as volatile and receding as 32.021 Bleu ciel. Ultramarine blue is the main pigment in both shades of color, but the "S" version of color shade 32.021 Bleu ciel is grayer, like an overcast sky. Substantial amounts of ocher and umber pigments added to the composition cloud the blue pigment.

18 See note 6 and 12 in the 1997 edition.
19 See note 6 and 12 in the second, modified 2006 edition.

CMYK approximation:
5.0.0.0

RGB approximation:
245.251.254

Spatial qualities:
passive, particularly effective
in the shade

Historical pigmentation:
china clay with lapis lazuli

Industrial pigmentation:
ultramarine blue with a very
neutral white

Facade suitability:
weather-resistant according
to the sort of ultramarine
pigment

08.003

Lapis lazuli blue / Bleu lapis-lazuli

Monika Meier, Chemist, 2008

Sodalite is a volcanic, translucent mineral that absorbs sulfur under certain geological conditions and transforms it into lapis lazuli crystals. "The Lapis lazuli stone has a magnificent color," wrote Gustav Tschermak in his textbook on mineralogy in 1894, "that arises from a sulfur bond. Found mixed with pyrite and limestone on the Lake Baikal, in Siberia, the Tartary, Bukhara, and Chile [sic]. The blue mineral containing pyrite particles was compared by the ancients to the starry sky."[20]
A later textbook on semi-precious stones points out that "the vitalizing blue of Lapis lazuli is endearing to the heart and to the eye of the beholder."[21] The interaction of lapis lazuli with light is enchanting and unique. The crystal surfaces in the natural stone absorb and reflect colors from surrounding objects, displaying them as colorful shadows on the light blue surface. This creates a subtle background for the daily color changes of the surroundings.

20 Translated from Gustav Tschermak, *Lehrbuch der Mineralogie* (Vienna, ⁴1894), p. 461.
21 Translated from Eduard Gübelin, *Edelsteine* (Zurich, 1969), p. 118.

CMYK approximation:
85.50.20.0

RGB approximation:
81.109.154

Spatial qualities:
dynamic

Historical pigmentation:
Cobalt-cerulean blue with
some chalk

Industrial pigmentation:
Phthalocyanine blue with
titanium white, green,
and red

Facade suitability:
not weather-resistant

32.030

Deep cerulean blue / Bleu ceruleum foncé

A shade of Le Corbusier's color palette from 1931 [22]

"A bare wall is a dead surface; a colorful wall comes to life. Transforming the wall by means of color will be one of the most fascinating problems of modern architecture. The problem of color has to be addressed on the level of the dynamic or static, decorative or destructive functionalities," wrote Fernand Léger, Le Corbusier's contemporary in the early 1920s in Paris. [23] Cerulean blue tends to the functionally dynamic colors, and ultramarine blue to the static. 32.020 Ultramarine blue 1931 is more receding than 32.030 Cerulean blue, which is equally dark in hue, but made with different pigments. The ultramarine series is comprised of cool, spiritual blue nuances. The cerulean blue series, which begins with this color, is comprised of warmer, less receding, and more greenish blue nuances.

22 Le Corbusier, 1959; Rüegg, 1997 (reprint, 2006).
23 Translated from Fernand Léger, quoted at the exhibtion
   Fernand Léger & Ideen für eine farbige Stadt,
   Centre Le Corbusier, Heidi Weber Haus (Zurich, 1970).

CMYK approximation:
45.0.20.0

RGB approximation:
170.208.210

Spatial qualities:
dynamic

Historical pigmentation:
Maya blue with chalk

Industrial pigmentation:
Cobalt blue, cobalt green,
red oxide, and titanium
white

Facade suitability:
weather-resistant

08.012

Turquoise / Turquoise

Gudrun Mende, color designer, 2008

A remarkably luminous, greenish-blue color adorned the temples of the Maya
of the Yucatán peninsula. The Indians knew how to heat indigo leaves and clay in
copal resin in order to produce Maya blue. The pigment was able to resist centuries
of erosion: Maya blue is still luminous in pre-Columbian frescoes, textiles, and
sculptures. Heating the ingredients allows the indigo to penetrate into the clay particles, thus increasing the lightfastness and brilliance of the indigo significantly.
It is believed that the pigment was produced during sacrificial rituals in vessels placed
in the embers, because it was seen as a symbol for the healing powers of rain—a
symbolism carried especially well by this watery, turquoise-blue pastel shade. Maya
blue was not available until quite recently. It is now one of the best quality blue
pigments available for exterior use.

CMYK approximation:
60.15.20.20

RGB approximation:
114.146.161

Spatial qualities:
dynamic

Historical pigmentation:
cobalt-cerulean blue with
chalk

Industrial pigmentation:
phthalocyanine blue with
titanium white

Facade suitability:
not weather-resistant

32.031

Bright cerulean blue / Bleu ceruleum vif

A shade of Le Corbusier's color palette from 1931[24]

Wassily Kandinsky touched upon a core issue in architecture with regard to color when he wrote that the distinction between the warm and cold quality of a color "occurs, so to speak, in the same plane, whereby the color keeps its basic character, but the character assumes a more material or immaterial quality. The movement is horizontal, with the warm colors shifting the plane towards the observer; the cold ones letting it retreat."[25] This differentiation is decisive when designing color concepts. Greenish-blue colors such as the ones in this series approach the viewer and create a sensual Mediterranean warmth. It has little in common with the reserved, mental quality of similarly dark ultramarine shades, other than the simple statement that they are both blue.

24 Le Corbusier, 1959; Rüegg, 1997 (reprint, 2006).
25 Translated from Wassily Kandinsky, *Über das Geistige in der Kunst* (Bern, 1952)
    (German original edition, 1910).

CMYK approximation:
50.10.20.0

RGB approximation:
156.188.198

Spatial qualities:
passive, also effective in
the shade

Historical pigmentation:
cobalt-cerulean blue
with chalk

Industrial pigmentation:
cobalt blue, chrome green,
titanium white, red oxide

Facade suitability:
weather-resistant

32.032

Medium cerulean blue 2 / Bleu ceruleum moyen 2

A shade of Le Corbusier's color palette from 1931 [26]

The aspect of being a warm (containing yellow) or a cold (containing blue) color
is decisive for its function. This distinction was made in Kandinsky's citation in the
previous text. Equally important as the warmth or coldness of a hue for its utility
in color design, which represents a *horizontal* shift, is its white content. From
one point of view, this sample is simply a lighter version of 32.031 Bleu ceruleum vif.
However, adding more white dramatically changes the dynamic quality of the color,
which is a *vertical* shift. The lighter shade is no longer dynamic, it stabilizes
itself in space. It no longer advances. It creates a warm, summery, airy atmosphere.
According to Kandinsky's logic, a blue's warmth or coldness can be recognized
as horizontal movement, and its lightness or dynamics as a vertical one.

26 Le Corbusier, 1931; Rüegg, 1997 (reprint, 2006).

CMYK approximation:
40.10.20.0

RGB approximation:
176.198.200

Spatial qualities:
passive, also effective in
the shade

Historical pigmentation:
cobalt-cerulean blue
with chalk

Industrial pigmentation:
cobalt blue, chrome green,
yellow oxide, and titanium
white

Facade suitability:
weather-resistant

32.033

Light cerulean blue / Bleu ceruleum clair

A shade of Le Corbusier's color palette from 1931 [27]

Le Corbusier assigned the third, even lighter version of the cerulean blue
pigment the mural value "sky". The mural values document a cultural significance
of certain pigments and colors. A cloudless summer sky reflected in the salty
water of the ocean forms the basis of a magnificent palette of greenish-blue shades.
The particles suspended in the ocean waves reflect the brilliant blue of the sky
in a special way. Le Corbusier assumed that colors such as this one would remind
most people of the summer sky. The suggestive power of such hues is often
made use of by advertisers, since so many people yearn for the sun and the sea.
This color stabilizes itself in space and subordinates itself to the forms and
the rhythm of architectural space.

27 Ibid.

CMYK approximation:
10.0.10.10

RGB approximation:
217.224.215

Spatial qualities:
passive, also effective in
the shade

Historical pigmentation:
cobalt-cerulean blue with
umber and chalk

Industrial pigmentation:
cobalt blue, chrome green,
yellow oxide, and titanium
white

Facade suitability:
weather-resistant

32.034

Pale cerulean blue / Bleu ceruleum pâle

A shade of Le Corbusier's color palette from 1931[28]

The lightest mixture of cobalt-cerulean blue is also the greenest, a green similar
to aquamarine blue and the color of water where the waves meet the shore and turn
into foam. If the color 32.033 recalls the reflection of the sky in water, 32.034 Bleu
ceruleum pâle recalls the cloudless sky reflected in sea foam. Le Corbusier also
categorized this nuance as "sky," thus differentiating between the two most important
blue pigments. The light ultramarine blue shades were assigned the mural value
"espace," which means space or infinity; the light cerulean blue shades were assigned
the mural value of "ciel", or sky. Thus, Le Corbusier distinguishes between a finite and
an infinite blue—between one that is earthbound, and one that is unlimited.

28 Ibid.

The Greens

By way of introduction to the final chapter dedicated to green colors, we begin with a short summary of the principles central to architectural color design, once color is regarded as a material, and material as the trigger for color perception.

- White surfaces and objects are immediately seen. This implies that their surroundings will seem darker and flatter than if seen against a less glaring white background.
- In contrast to this, surfaces and objects will move to the background if they are painted with gray. Designers place things in the shadows by painting them gray. Graying chromatic colors with their complementary color will achieve the same effect, while also making it easier to create harmonious relationships with other colors.
- Leafing metal pigments reflect light and maintain their noble character even in spaces with low light. This is quite the opposite with yellow colors, since bright yellow pigments require the most high-energy light and will seem gloomy in dark spaces.
- Colors made from ocher pigments with their inherent content of gray generally look more luminous in dark spaces than yellows.
- Red, orange, and yellow are "daughters of the light," since they will unfold their richest beauty in full light.
- Blue, gray, and black are "daughters of the night," they are located at the other pole of the color designer's axis of light and shadow colors, they are most effective in low light conditions.
- Yellow surfaces advance, and colors with a yellow content will advance in space more than similar colors without yellow.
- Red objects are assertive and substantial, blue objects on the contrary are more ethereal. Pure red and pure blue form the extreme poles of the mass axis.

These principles can be illustrated as shown:

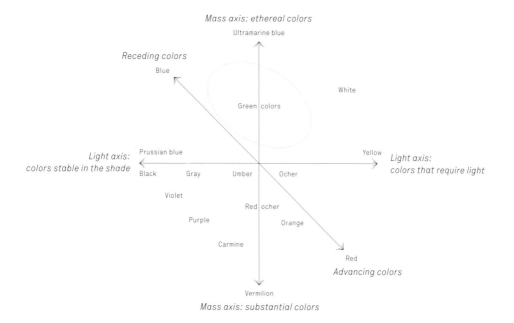

The often-mentioned ambivalence of green colors can be explained with reference to this illustration. Since they can either advance and recede or require high levels of light or be stable in the shade, they need to be divided into two subgroups. Greens containing yellow will advance in space, as do all colors on the right side of the illustration, and they also need strong light in order to be luminous. These are the sprouting greens of spring. Greens containing blue, on the other hand, will recede, they are more stable under all light conditions, and can be compared to the muted green palette of evergreen trees.

> "First, we will concentrate on isolated colors, letting a single color affect us.
> We are looking for a scheme that is as straightforward as can be, one that can be reduced to its simplest form.
> The two great divisions that strike us immediately are:
> The warmth and coldness of the color and
> The lightness and darkness of the same.
> Now we have arrived at 4 possibilities for each color: it is I. warm and either 1. light or 2. dark, or it is II. cold and either 1. light or 2. dark.
> The warmth or coldness of a color is its general tendency to yellow or to blue. This differentiation is made in the same plane, so to speak, thus the color keeps its basic character [green, for instance] but the character is either more material or more immaterial. The movement is a horizontal one, whereby the warm aspect shifts the plane towards the viewer, the cold makes it retreats away from him. [...]
> This effect is amplified when the light and dark difference is added: the effect of yellow is strengthened when it is lightened (put simply: when white is added). The effect of blue is strengthened when it is darkened (adding black)."
> *Wassily Kandinsky* [1]

If green colors are discriminated according to these criteria, they will lose their ambivalence, and the selection of the most beautiful green for a surface will be crowned with success.

1 Translated from Wassily Kandinsky, *Über das Geistige in der Kunst* (Bern, 1952), p. 87–88 (original edition 1910).

CMYK approximation:
90.0.20.90

RGB approximation:
11.28.33

Spatial qualities:
dynamic, effective even in
low light conditions

Historical pigmentation:
English green with bone black

Industrial pigmentation:
chrome green with black

Facade suitability:
weather-resistant

26.040

Black green / Vert noir

Villa La Roche (Le Corbusier, Pierre Jeanneret), 1923–1925

This is the color of the slightly glossy, dark green coniferous needles of the pine tree, a color rich in symbolism in Japanese art. The dark green needles of the pine are credited with "the power of driving demons away."[2] The evergreen symbolizes unwavering determination and empowered maturation. Japanese art understood how to emphasize the exceptional quality of Black green by often combining it with lacquered gold. A similar idea was pursued in the staircase of the Villa La Roche in Paris. The hand railings painted with Black green oil paint were capped with simple, heavy brass orbs. The interplay of the shiny brass orbs, the black stone steps, and the creamy walls coated with chalk is delightful and effective.

2 Lafcadio Hearn, "In a Japanese Garden," *Atlantic Monthly*,
July 1892, p. 14–33.

CMYK approximation:
100.0.25.60

RGB approximation:
26.80.94

Spatial qualities:
dynamic, luminous in low light
conditions

Historical pigmentation:
ultramarine green

Industrial pigmentation:
ultramarine green cannot be
reproduced well

Facade suitability:
not weather-resistant

04.004

Ultramarine green / Vert outremer

Hans Kittel, color chart of chips made with ultramarine pigments, 1953[3]

Ultramarine green is a sulfur-reduced relative of its famous blue brother. Ultramarine blue evolves from heating of 100 kg of china clay, 116 kg of sodium sulfate, 20 kg of charcoal. If 26 kg of charcoal are used, then the chemically closely related blue-green pigment called ultramarine green results. Fifty percent of the raw mixture is lost during the pigment purification process. This low yield explains why the beautiful pigment played such a subordinate role in the history of painting. The striking, enigmatic effect and the fascination associated with ultramarine blue are still present in Ultramarine green. Since any color made with ultramarines is effective and will show a salient luminosity under low light conditions, and since Ultramarine green is actually more blue than green, it serves architecture well on surfaces that would not function well with a deep green color tending towards yellow.

3 Hans Kittel, *Taschenbuch der Farben- und Werkstoffkunde*
(Stuttgart, 1953).

CMYK approximation:
70.20.60.0

RGB approximation:
112.157.127

Spatial qualities:
dynamic

Historical pigmentation:
hydrated chromium oxide with
baryte

Industrial pigmentation:
phthalocyanine green,
blue tint with titanium white

Facade suitability:
not weather-resistant

43.7

Bright green / Vert vif

A shade of Le Corbusier's color palette from 1959 [4]

An enamel made with the cool, emerald-green pigment hydrated chromium oxide
once decorated the signs of all British Petroleum gas stations. The unique color of
this pigment, also known as chrome green fiery, Guigent's green, or viridian green,
is produced when chromium oxide green, the standard, dull green color of many early
industrial machines, includes water in its crystal structures. It was always an
expensive pigment, but, when added to barium sulfate as substrate to make permanent
green, a green color was produced that surpassed organic pigments in terms of
luminosity and lightfastness. Le Corbusier liked this color so much that he included it
in his 1959 color scale, which consisted of only twenty colors. An oil paint in this
color was used to contrast with oak and burnt Sienna oil paints on the fronts of the
kitchen cabinets in the Unité d'Habitation in Marseilles.

4 Le Corbusier, *Claviers de Couleurs Salubra 2* (Basel, 1959).
See also Arthur Rüegg (ed.), *Polychromie architecturale. Le Corbusiers Farbenklaviaturen von 1931 und 1959 /
Le Corbusier's Color Keyboards from 1931 and 1959 / Les claviers de couleurs de Le Corbusier de 1931 et de 1959*
(Basel, Boston, Berlin, 1997) (reprint, 2006).

CMYK approximation:
70.10.50.40

RGB approximation:
77.113.99

Spatial qualities:
dynamic, effective also in
low light conditions

Historical pigmentation:
Victoria green, later cobalt
green deep with red ocher

Industrial pigmentation:
cobalt or phthalocyanine
green muted

Facade suitability:
weather-resistant in some
techniques

32.040

Deep green / Vert foncé

A shade of Le Corbusier's color palette from 1931[5]

The series of greens tending towards blue, which begins with Vert foncé, is the counterpoint to Le Corbusier's sap green series of shades tending towards yellow. The color shades of the sap green series are more dynamic, more sensitive to low lighting, and they advance slightly in space. The series of greens with blue in them, ranging from 32.040 to 32.042, contains colors that are calm, reserved, and cool. They stabilize themselves in space and love the shade. They speak of the muted sounds of the forest and of the elegance of an English interior. Le Corbusier called this color "vert anglais," meaning the pigment Victoria green, a composite of zinc yellow, viridian green, and barium sulfate. Victoria green was used to make the noble enamel for British racing cars and to pigment a beloved oil paint for use in fine art, on wood, and on steel. Le Corbusier appreciated the aristocratic color and liked to use it both in interiors and on exteriors.

5 Le Corbusier, *Claviers de Couleurs Salubra* (Basel, 1931).
 See also Arthur Rüegg (ed.), *Polychromie architecturale. Le Corbusiers Farbenklaviaturen von 1931 und 1959 / Le Corbusier's Color Keyboards from 1931 and 1959 / Les claviers de couleurs de Le Corbusier de 1931 et de 1959* (Basel, Boston, Berlin, 1997) (reprint, 2006).

CMYK approximation:
30.0.25.15

RGB approximation:
175.195.180

Spatial qualities:
passive, effective even in
low light conditions

Historical pigmentation:
cobalt green with red ocher
and chalk

Industrial pigmentation:
cobalt green with oxide
pigments and white.

Facade suitability:
weather-resistant

32.041

Veronese green / Vert Véronèse

A shade of Le Corbusier's color palette from 1931[6]

Adding white to Victoria green created beautiful medium, muted green nuances such as this one. The lightfastness of such mixtures was excellent, and wallpaper manufacturers were happy to make use of them to produce high-quality wallpaper. The name of the color, Veronese green, is slightly confusing because it refers to two completely different greens. The dull pigment from Verona contains celadonite; it is grayer and more austere. Colors such as 32.044 Gray green or 32.043 Rüegg green at most can be produced with this pigment. The Venetian Renaissance painter Paolo Veronese (1528–1588) was known for using a particular grayish-green middle tone, which was given his name. Le Corbusier's bluish-green Vert Véronèse is in between. It is not made from a green earth pigment, but it is also grayer, calmer, and more receding than standard Veronese green mixtures. After all, Le Corbusier's color had to harmonize with other colors.

6 Ibid.

CMYK approximation:
15.0.20.10

RGB approximation:
209.218.198

Spatial qualities:
passive, effective even in
low light conditions

Historical pigmentation:
cobalt green deep with red
ocher and chalk

Industrial pigmentation:
cobalt green with oxide
pigments and white.

Facade suitability:
weather-resistant

32.042

Light Veronese green / Vert Véronèse clair

A shade of Le Corbusier's color palette from 1931[7]

This is a low-key grayish green similar in color to the back side of evergreen coniferous needles. Vert Véronèse clair builds a quiet bridge to the landscape. In the housing development at Pessac (Le Corbusier, Pierre Jeanneret, 1925–1928), Le Corbusier was able to camouflage some of the houses' walls by using the color numbered "42 = vert anglais + blanc,"[8] a lime paint in this shade. The color concept for the Frugès housing development in Pessac was realized at about the same time the first Salubra color collection was published. The other colors of the Frugès concept were: 1 = blanc (corresponds to the shade 32.001), 12 = noir et blanc (32.012), 23 = outremer et blanc (32.023), 91 = rouge vermillon et blanc (32.091), 112 = rouge anglais et blanc (32.112), 120 = terre sienne brûlée (32.120) und 130 = terre d'ombre brûlée (32.130). Combining the serene green with warm red earth colors enhances its tranquil effect.

7 Ibid.
8 M. Ferrand, J.-P. Feugas, B. Le Roy, J.-L. Veyret, *Le Corbusier: Les Quartiers Modernes Frugès* (Paris, Basel, Boston, Berlin, 1998), p. 131.

CMYK approximation:
40.0.35.20

RGB approximation:
150.178.155

Spatial qualities:
dynamic, effective even in
low light conditions

Historical pigmentation:
Paris green imitation made
from phthalocyanine
green, chalk, and red ocher

Industrial pigmentation:
cobalt green with yellow and
red iron oxide.

Facade suitability:
weather-resistant

20-30.8

Light green / Vert clair

Photographic material from the archives of the Fondation Le Corbusier

This warmer version of the color 32.041 was tracked down in the archives of the
Fondation Le Corbusier in Paris by its former director, Evelyne Tréhin. She maintained
that this green was used for certain facade elements of the Frugès housing estate
in Pessac. This assumption is not shared by some other experts. It is, however,
a fact that greens mixed with four colors such as this one harmonize with deep reds
and browns and with natural wood. For decades, highly toxic pigments containing
arsenic were used to produce similar shades of color. Lightened versions of the two
copper arsenate pigments, Scheele's green and Paris green, produce a color such
as Vert clair. They were both appreciated as wallpaper paints, until the English
government sounded the alarm in 1860 and called for non-toxic synthetic pigments.

CMYK approximation:
20.5.30.5

RGB approximation:
206.215.184

Spatial qualities:
dynamic, effective even in
low light conditions

Historical pigmentation:
cobalt green with chalk and
red ocher

Industrial pigmentation:
cobalt green with yellow and
red iron oxide.

Facade suitability:
weather-resistant

32.043

Rüegg green / Vert Rüegg

Arthur Rüegg, architect, 2003

This elegant, greenish-gray nuance, reminiscent of the petals of the Carline
thistle, is calm and stable in space: a color of understatement with a typical history.
Arthur Rüegg and his team planned to paint the back wall of an open staircase
with Le Corbusier's 32.090 Rouge foncé. An adjacent wall was to be painted with
32.042 Vert Véronèse clair. However, Rouge foncé was too aggressive. Adding green
and red pigments darkened the red without compromising its strength and created
the color now called 32.095 Swiss red. In this combination 32.042 Vert Véronèse
was too cool. Adding raw Sienna muted the green beautifully and gave the staircase
a new elegance that the architects liked very much. Rüegg green also goes very
well with chrome and glass kitchens.

CMYK approximation:
10.10.35.5

RGB approximation:
220.214.172

Spatial qualities:
passive and stable under
all light conditions

Historical pigmentation:
Veronese green with
Champagne chalk

Industrial pigmentation:
chrome green, iron oxide
and white

Facade suitability:
weather-resistant

32.044

Green gray / Vert gris

Hans Kittel, color chart of earth colors, 1953[9]

The European standard color assortment before the Second World War included
only one natural green color: green earth. The various names given the weathering
products of green rocks reflect their geographical origins, such as Tyrolean
green, Bohemian green, Veronese green, and stone green. The rare Veronese green
earth from Monte Baldo on Lake Garda had a clear blue hue, and was the most
expensive of all green earths. Bohemian green was less blue and warmer. When lightened with Champagne chalk it creates a grayish-green color that is dignified
and discrete. This calming grayish green has a long history of use as a wall paint
in English interiors. Like other hues that are heavily muted, this shade is pleasant
in dark rooms. It is a color that gives "all other neighboring colors a subdued,
coherent quality."[10]

9 Kittel, 1953
10 Max Doerner, *Malmaterial und seine Verwendung im Bilde*
   (Stuttgart, 1994).

CMYK approximation:
20.0.65.5

RGB approximation:
205.218.125

Spatial qualities:
dynamic

Historical pigmentation:
chrome green muted with
chalk and ocher

Industrial pigmentation:
complex pigment mixture

Facade suitability:
weather-resistant in some
techniques

06.034

Green tea / Thé vert

A color of the Baumann Prase color card from 1912 [11]

Ogden Rood, the author of the book *Die Moderne Farbenlehre* [12] from 1880,
was of the opinion that green itself was not difficult to use in designs, but that it was
difficult, when using coloring materials, to successfully convey the quality of green
to a surface. Rood believed that this was due to the gentle and subtle color interplay
of natural green nuances. Natural greens are, in fact, never monochromatic; they
are complex, pointillist images consisting of numerous, more or less green nuances.
Analyzed more closely, nature offers an array of pale gray to strongly yellow-green
tones. It is the multi-facetted interplay of the many shades all observed together that
makes a green beautiful and significant in a meadow or on leaves. If this spectacle
is memorized and a particular green is selected and used to paint a whole surface, it
is bound to look much brighter, more glaring and artificial than it did in nature. Artificial
grass, and also most other green colors, suffer the same consequence, whereas
Green tea, with its multi-colored components, looks modern and natural.

11 Otto Prase, *Baumanns Neue Farbtonkarten System Prase*
   (Aue/Saxony, 1912).
12 Ogden N. Rood, *Die Moderne Farbenlehre*
   (Leipzig, 1880).

CMYK approximation:
20.10.50.10

RGB approximation:
193.196.136

Spatial qualities:
passive

Historical pigmentation:
chrome green muted
with chalk

Industrial pigmentation:
complex pigment mixture

Facade suitability:
weather-resistant in some
techniques

08.009

Lux Guyer Saffa 11.5 / Vert Saffa 11.5

A color in Lux Guyer's Saffa house, 1928 [13]

The history of women in architecture was long a history of absence. It has become clear though that many of the practical rural homes built before 1900 in the United States were designed by women. These women provided for a large kitchen, a veranda, good ventilation, a ground level bedroom for the elderly or infirmed, and an adequate servant's room.[14] Conforming to similar ideas and staying within the tradition of the English country house, the Schweizerische Austellung für Frauenarbeit (Saffa; Swiss exhibition of women's work) exhibited a practical, "comfortable medium-sized house" in 1928. Designed by Lux Guyer (1894–1955), the first independent female architect in Switzerland, it was one of the first prefabricated houses constructed of wood. Principles concerned with the requirements of family life were central to the design. The playful color concept supported functional, tranquil living areas by using heavily muted yellows, blues, and greens, such as this very pleasant green. The prefabricated wooden house was conceived so that it could be built in only three weeks.[15]

13 Verein proSAFFAhaus, Institut für Geschichte und Theorie der Architektur der ETH Zürich (eds.),
    Die drei Leben des Saffa-Hauses. Lux Guyers Musterhaus von 1928 (Zurich, 1928).
14 Jackie Craven, "Forgotten Women Designers. Women Have Always Played a Role in Home Design,"
    http://architecture.about.com/od/greatarchitects/a/forgotten.htm (December 7, 2009).
15 The house was reconstructed in 2006 in Stäfa on Lake Zurich from original components,
    after it had been in Aarau from 1928 to 2003.

CMYK approximation:
15.0.100.25

RGB approximation:
174.182.30

Spatial qualities:
dynamic, nuance responds
strongly to light

Historical pigmentation:
zinc green made from
zinc yellow and Prussian
blue with ocher

Industrial pigmentation:
cobalt green with yellow iron
oxide

Facade suitability:
weather-resistant

43.6

Olive green / Vert olive

A shade of Le Corbusier's color palette from 1959 [16]

Le Corbusier included this green, similar to the color of the leaves of the reseda medicinal plant, in his later color scale. The origins of this interesting color can be traced back to a method that artists traditionally employed to mix olive greens from brownish ochers and green synthetic mineral colors such as zinc green (during Le Corbusier's lifetime) or cobalt green. An English color theory, which has been forgotten over time, says that a color will achieve a harmonious effect if it contains elements of all three primary colors.[17] Mixtures of natural ocher and zinc green pigments guarantee this harmony, and it could explain why Vert olive transcends the spectrum of architecturally hard-to-use, volatile green shades. What is unique about this color is its shift in changing daylight from a straw-colored, luminous yellow with a green hue to a strongly yellow, pleasant green.

16 Le Corbusier, 1959; Rüegg, 1997 (reprint, 2006).
17 George Field, *The Rudiments of Colour and Colouring* (London, 1870).

CMYK approximation:
75.20.80.20

RGB approximation:
82.127.80

Spatial qualities:
dynamic, nuance responds
strongly to light

Historical pigmentation:
chrome green made from
chrome yellow and Prussian
blue

Industrial pigmentation:
cobalt green with red oxide

Facade suitability:
weather-resistant in some
techniques

32.050

Bright green / Vert vif 2

A shade of Le Corbusier's color palette from 1931[18]

Bright green is the deepest and most neutral green on Le Corbusier's color scale. In the 1930s, there were many high-quality opaque colors made from Prussian blue and chrome yellow mixtures commercially available. Product names such as leaf green, sap green, vermilion green (a very luminous green), and chariot green point to the highly functional value of green mixtures, but also to the reference of these nuances to the greens we see in landscape. One of Le Corbusier's keyboards for the first Salubra color collection is based on the nuances of this green series and is called "paysage—landscape." The landscape green colors in the series range from 32.050 Vert vif 2 to 32.053 Vert pâle, the gentle green of young sprouts. They look their best in good light conditions. In semi-darkness or at dusk, the colors in nature as well as those in this landscape green series lose some of their luminosity.

18 Le Corbusier, 1931; Rüegg, 1997 (reprint, 2006).

CMYK approximation:
45.0.70.10

RGB approximation:
152.187.111

Spatial qualities:
dynamic, nuance responds
strongly to light

Historical pigmentation:
chrome green made from
chrome yellow and Prussian
blue lightened

Industrial pigmentation:
titanium white, cobalt green
and bismuth yellow

Facade suitability:
weather-resistant in some
techniques

32.051

Medium green / Vert moyen

A shade of Le Corbusier's color palette from 1931[19]

Although the green colors in nature continually change with the seasons, they never come close to the pure green color of the rainbow. Pale-colored greens in winter and gentle springtime greens increase their yellow content and gain luminosity, first becoming lush, yellowish-green, then succulent green, to finally replace their green content with red in the fall. The basic green color takes on successive tinges of yellow, orange, red, and brown, in that order. Le Corbusier's landscape green series follows the same logic: Vert moyen, actually a sap green, contains much more yellow than the previous midsummer green, and the next lighter color in the series will have an even higher level of yellow, thus creating the inner balance that nature achieves year after year as a matter of course. Le Corbusier's Medium green is striking, it advances in space, and is dynamic. Combinations with strong ultramarine blue tones increase this dynamic, while combinations with the harmonious umbers will calm it.

19 Ibid.

CMYK approximation:
40.0.70.0

RGB approximation:
175.208.121

Spatial qualities:
dynamic, nuance responds
strongly to light

Historical pigmentation:
zinc green mixed with
complementary colors and
lightened

Industrial pigmentation:
titanium white, cobalt green
and bismuth yellow

Facade suitability:
weather-resistant in some
techniques

32.052

Green yellow / Vert jaune

A shade of Le Corbusier's color palette from 1931 [20]

The color Le Corbusier specified as 32.052 Vert jaune contains an almost
imperceptible amount of red. For technical reasons, green paints mixed by machine
according to color software never contain red. This is the difference between
conventional yellowish-green colors as shown in the many color finders on the one
hand, and the greens designed by Le Corbusier and their forerunners in nature
on the other. Natural greens, as they require copper for growth, always contain at
least a small amount of a red pigment. Conventional statements concerning light
green colors do not apply to colors produced with red content, such as Vert jaune.
Vert jaune does not make faces look sallow, thus it works well in living rooms.
Vert jaune contains elements of all the springtime greens of nature and reminds
us gently of the energy inherent to sprouting and growth.

20 Ibid.

CMYK approximation:
20.0.45.0

RGB approximation:
216.230.170

Spatial qualities:
dynamic, nuance responds
strongly to light

Historical pigmentation:
chrome green made from
chrome yellow and Prussian
blue lightened

Industrial pigmentation:
titanium white, cobalt green
and bismuth yellow

Facade suitability:
weather-resistant in some
techniques

32.053

Pale green / Vert pâle

A shade of Le Corbusier's color palette from 1931 [21]

The optimistic landscape green series of the 1920s comes to its temporary end
with this silvery-gray, yellowish green. It corresponds to the color of tender shoots of
grass after the first rays of the spring sun. Like the sprouting grass, the nuance
is both fragile and earthy, and thus balanced. These qualities allow it to be used in a
variety of situations. In our work with the colors of this green scale, which ranges
from 32.050 to 32.053, we noticed that they look significantly more spirited on vertical
surfaces than on small samples. To achieve the desired effect, it is advisable to
choose the lighter nuance when the darker one shown previously, 32.052 Vert jaune,
was actually selected. The darker the space, the more important is this premise.

21 Ibid.

This publication was kindly supported by:
kt.COLOR www.ktcolor.com
Karl Bubenhofer AG www.kabe-farben.ch
Thymos www.thymos.ch

Library of Congress Control Number: 2010923971

Bibliographic information published by the Deutsche Nationalbibliothek
The Deutsche Nationalbibliothek lists this publication in the
Deutsche Nationalbibliografie; detailed bibliographic data are available
on the Internet at http://dnb.d-nb.de.

This book is also available in a German language edition:
128 Farben. Ein Musterbuch für Architekten, Denkmalpfleger und Gestalter
(ISBN: 978-3-0346-0315-7)

www.birkhauser-architecture.com

© 2010 Birkhäuser GmbH
Basel
P.O. Box 133, CH-4010 Basel,
Switzerland

Translation into English:
Laura Bruce, Berlin
Project management:
Karoline Mueller-Stahl, Leipzig
Layout and cover design:
Muriel Comby, Basel

Printed on acid-free paper
produced from chlorine-free pulp.
TCF ∞
Printed in Germany

ISBN: 978-3-0346-0317-1

9 8 7 6 5 4 3 2 1